THE SNOWDONIA WAY

by Alex Kendall

2 POLICE SQUARE, MILNTHORPE, CUMBRIA LA7 7PY
www.cicerone.co.uk

Printed by KHL Printing, Singapore
A catalogue record for this book is available from the British Library.
All photographs are by the author unless otherwise stated.

Acknowledgements

I'd like to thank Jenny Wilson and Emily Stachowiak, who came with me to walk sections of the book, through pleasant days and not-so-pleasant bogs and hailstorms. I'd also like to thank Rosemary Moorhouse-Gann and Monica Kendall who helped me check the whole route and made sure the directions made sense. Finally, a huge thanks for the advice and information I've been given by countless friends, café workers, hostel staff members and people in the hills.

Updates to this guide

While every effort is made by our authors to ensure the accuracy of guidebooks as they go to print, changes can occur during the lifetime of an edition. Any updates that we know of for this guide will be on the Cicerone website (www.cicerone.co.uk/856/updates), so please check before planning your trip. We also advise that you check information about such things as transport, accommodation and shops locally. Even rights of way can be altered over time.

We are always grateful for information about any discrepancies between a guidebook and the facts on the ground, sent by email to updates@cicerone.co.uk or by post to Cicerone, 2 Police Square, Milnthorpe LA7 7PY, United Kingdom.

Front cover: Looking north from the summit of Cadair Idris (Stage 1B)

CONTENTS

Warning

Mountain walking can be a dangerous activity carrying a risk of personal injury or death. It should be undertaken only by those with a full understanding of the risks and with the training and experience to evaluate them. While every care and effort has been taken in the preparation of this guide, the user should be aware that conditions can be highly variable and can change quickly, materially affecting the seriousness of a mountain walk. Therefore, except for any liability that cannot be excluded by law, neither Cicerone nor the author accept liability for damage of any nature (including damage to property, personal injury or death) arising directly or indirectly from the information in this book.

To call out the Mountain Rescue, ring 999 or the international emergency number 112: this will connect you via any available network. Once connected to the emergency operator, ask for the police.

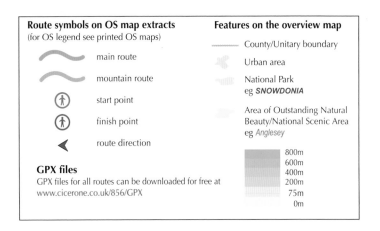

Route symbols on OS map extracts
(for OS legend see printed OS maps)

~~~~~ main route

~~~~~ mountain route

(🏃) start point

(🏃) finish point

◀ route direction

GPX files

GPX files for all routes can be downloaded for free at www.cicerone.co.uk/856/GPX

Features on the overview map

--------- County/Unitary boundary

Urban area

National Park
eg **SNOWDONIA**

Area of Outstanding Natural Beauty/National Scenic Area
eg *Anglesey*

800m
600m
400m
200m
75m
0m

Public transport links

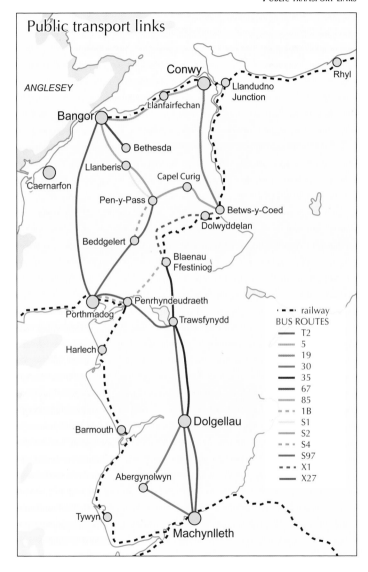

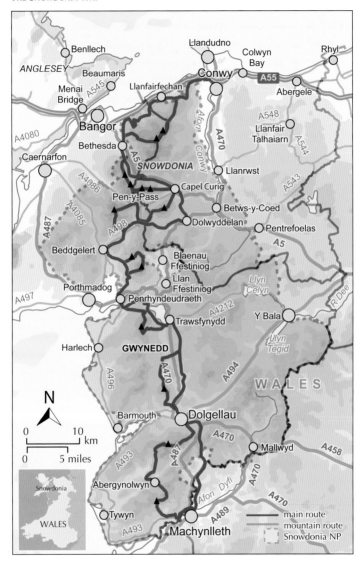

ROUTE SUMMARY TABLE

Stage	Distance	Ascent	Approx time	Page
Main route				
1 Machynlleth to Dolgellau	15½ miles (24.7km)	2460ft (750m)	7–8hr	32
2 Dolgellau to Trawsfynydd	14 miles (22.6km)	2590ft (790m)	7hr	61
3 Trawsfynydd to Beddgelert	18½ miles (29.5km)	3050ft (930m)	8–9hr	80
4 Beddgelert to Dolwyddelan	12¾ miles (20.6km)	2625ft (800m)	6–7hr	107
5 Dolwyddelan to Bethesda	15½ miles (25.1km)	2165ft (660m)	7–8hr	130
6 Bethesda to Conwy	21 miles (33.6km)	4855ft (1480m)	10–11hr	146
Total	**97¼ miles (156.1km)**	**17,745ft (5410m)**	**45–50hr**	
Mountain route				
1A Machynlleth to Abergynolwyn	12 miles (19.5km)	3575ft (1090m)	6–7hr	45
1B Abergynolwyn to Dolgellau	14¾ miles (23.6km)	4890ft (1490m)	8hr	53
2A Dolgellau to Trawsfynydd	16½ miles (26.6km)	4560ft (1390m)	9hr	71
3A Trawsfynydd to Penrhyndeudraeth	11¾ miles (18.9km)	2855ft (870m)	6–7hr	92
3B Penrhyndeudraeth to Beddgelert	15¾ miles (25.2km)	4495ft (1370m)	7–8hr	99
4A Beddgelert to Pen-y-Pass	11¼ miles (17.9km)	4855ft (1480m)	6–7hr	117
4B Pen-y-Pass to Capel Curig	9½ miles (15.5km)	4165ft (1270m)	5–6hr	124
5A Capel Curig to Bethesda	12¾ miles (20.4km)	5380ft (1640m)	7–8hr	
6A Bethesda to Conwy	18 miles (28.7km)	5215ft (1590m)	9–10hr	156
Total	**122¼ miles (196.3km)**	**39990ft (12,190m)**	**63–70hr**	

The Afon Ogwen and Y Garn (Stage 5)

INTRODUCTION

Snowdonia, an area encompassing the mountains of North Wales, is a wild expanse of peaks, valleys, woodland, and miles of coastline and estuaries. In a short distance you can walk from the sandy beaches of Tremadoc Bay, through the forested river gorge of Aberglaslyn Pass, up to the flanks of Snowdon itself – the highest mountain in the land. It is a landscape forged by the heat of volcanoes and the long slow movement of ice, a land that has seen druids, Roman invasion, the shadow of King Arthur, and the great Welsh princes, who made this mountainous country an independent land long after others had fallen.

The Snowdonia Way is a long-distance walking trail that takes you the full length of the National Park, from Machynlleth in the south to Conwy in the north, between the two great rivers that mark the southern and eastern edges of the region, the Dyfi and the Conwy. For 97 miles (156km), walked in six days, you'll see the many sides of Snowdonia, and explore its nature and history with the option of summiting some peaks. There are good

The entrance to Ogwen Valley is dominated by Gallt yr Ogof (Stage 5)

11

transport links in all the towns and villages passed through, meaning you can attempt the whole route in one go, or split it up as you see fit – perhaps even doing one day at a time over the years!

The main route

The main route is primarily low level, taking valley tracks and hillside paths, encountering old rights of way through forested slopes, and even using Roman roads. There are some steep ascents and descents to encounter, but the route avoids the peaks, meaning it can be walked by those wishing for a journey through the landscape, gazing up at the mountains but enjoying the feeling of being in the valleys.

On this route you'll walk for hours in some of the most stunning mountain scenery in the UK, come across surprising remains from our industrial past, see wildlife and waterfalls, and of course get to sample some excellent pubs and cafés with the great people who call this place home.

As the only long-distance low-level route through Snowdonia, the Snowdonia Way is the best way to get to know this part of the world. You'll see the most famous sights, from the great northern cliffs of Cadair Idris to the pass of Aberglaslyn, the Ogwen Valley and Aber Falls. Of course the route can't include all the paths of Snowdonia, but hopefully you'll be tempted to come back and explore more.

The mountain route

For those who want to climb some mountains on the way, a high-level route has also been devised. This route intersects with the standard route regularly, so you can switch between them when you feel like it or when the weather dictates, or you can walk the whole high-level route from beginning to end. This route is 122 miles (196km) in total and is done in nine stages, also between Machynlleth and Conwy.

The high-level route names have a letter in them; for example, Stage 2 has an alternative high-level route called Stage 2A. Where the high route takes more than one stage to get to the end point of the corresponding low-level route stage, it is split into two letters; for example, Stage 3 (low-level) has a high-level route that is Stage 3A and then Stage 3B.

Although many of the overnight stops are the same, there are a few instances where they do not quite overlap. The only night, however, where the high-level route spends the night far from any intersection with the low-level route, is after Stage 1A in Abergynolwyn. Other than that, it is relatively easy to swap between them when you see fit.

This route gives you a spectacular journey over Snowdonia's mountains, climbing the most famous peaks such as Snowdon, Cadair Idris, Cnicht and the Glyders, and also taking you to some of the peaks less visited, which you may have all to yourself.

SNOWDON (YR WYDDFA – 'THE TUMULUS')

Looking south from Snowdon's summit (Stage 4A)

Snowdon is a mountain cloaked in myths and legends, many of which concern King Arthur. He was said to have fought his final battle on the slopes of Cwm Llan, where he was killed by a hail of arrows from Bwlch y Saethau ('the pass of arrows'). Glaslyn has also been named among the possible lakes Arthur's sword Excalibur was thrown into by Sir Bedivere after Arthur's death, and the peak of Y Lliwedd is said to contain a cave where the knights of the Round Table lie sleeping, waiting to rise again and fight at Britain's hour of need.

The Welsh name of the mountain, Yr Wyddfa, also relates to King Arthur. He is said to have killed the giant Rhitta Gawr and buried him on the summit. Yr Wyddfa means 'the tumulus' or 'the burial cairn' after this story, whereas the English 'Snowdon' comes from the old English 'snaw' and 'dun', meaning snow hill. Many of these features have alternative and equally interesting interpretations, such as that about Bwlch y Saethau being where hunters (with bows and arrows) would watch for deer, but the myths lend a fantastic backdrop to any day out.

For hundreds of years Snowdon has been a popular destination for walkers and climbers. From the 17th to 19th centuries it was the destination for several well-known botanists on tours to collect mountain plants, and as well as other rare species it is one of the only places in Britain where

13

the Snowdon lily can be found. Because of its alpine flora, the mountain has been designated a national nature reserve, and is protected accordingly. Alongside the botanists and generations of climbers, it was used by the successful 1953 Everest expedition for training, while they stayed in the Pen y Gwryd hotel near Pen y Pass. Snowdon is now possibly the most climbed mountain in Britain due to its accessibility, height, large number of routes, and the incredible views from the summit.

It is impossible to give a full account of the rich history and nature of Snowdon in this short book, so interested readers should read up more about this fantastic mountain. See Appendix D for suggestions for further reading about the area.

LANDSCAPE

What you see when you look out over Snowdonia on a clear day is a landscape that has been through thousands of years of differing human uses. Today some of these are more prevalent than others, some we look back on with dismay and some with fondness.

The forests began to be cleared in the Stone Age. In the warmer and drier climate of the time, trees would have been high up on the mountains, and the combination of a move to a colder and wetter climate, linked to the introduction of cattle and goats, would have prevented their regrowth.

The south ridge of Snowdon (Stage 4A)

Copper, lead and some iron were mined right up to the Roman invasion in the first century CE, forts were built, and the natural forests got smaller.

Sheep farming on the hills is a relatively recent introduction, having grown over the last few hundred years, largely replacing cattle and goats. The bald, grassy look of many of the hills is down to grazing pressure by sheep, which reduces biodiversity and prevents the regrowth of trees. Sheep farming has been the dominant industry in Snowdonia and a vital occupation for thousands of people, providing both wool and lamb. There has recently been a move to reduce some grazing pressure to allow natural regrowth of plants, which can clearly be seen in protected areas such as on Cadair Idris and Cwm Idwal, which was Wales' first nature reserve.

Interrupting the dominance of sheep farming in shaping the landscape was the mining and quarrying of slate, which experienced a huge boom from the 18th to 20th centuries. Slate in North Wales is mudstone and shale that has been put under immense pressure and so can be split cleanly down one side, forming sheets. It has mostly been used in building (notably for roof tiles), and at the peak of production it was shipped round the world. The remains of many slate workings can be seen in the landscape, and the great spoil tips are slowly being recolonised by vegetation.

The last of the three major landscape-changing industries to affect Snowdonia was forestry, where vast areas of the uplands were afforested by the Forestry Commission,

The ruins of the old slate mines in Cwm Llan (Stage 4A)

established in 1919 to deal with a national wood shortage. Most of the original plantations were ugly shapes, were less biodiverse and used non-native conifers from North America. Nowadays the Forestry Commission is far more sympathetic to conservation of wildlife, and of shaping forests to fit into the landscape.

Today we see not a static landscape but a dynamic, ever-changing one. A National Park since 1951 (and one of the UK's first), Snowdonia's priorities are always changing as tastes and markets come and go, and as people visit for different reasons. The National Park Authority has a huge task in trying to balance the conservation of nature, the interests of the visitors who come to enjoy the natural beauty, and the needs of the people who live in the Park and whose livelihoods are bound up in the landscape.

PLANTS AND WILDLIFE

The varied habitats of Snowdonia create the conditions for the existence of a wide range of wild animals and plants. Where cliffs are too steep or sheep have been excluded there are many flowering plants, and those high up on the mountainsides feature true arctic-alpine species such as purple saxifrage. Snowdonia is the furthest south in Britain that many of these species reach, reflecting a gradual retreat north after the end of the last ice age.

The most common flowers you are likely to see include the small yellow flowers of tormentil, the milky pale primrose, and the purple flowers of common dog violet and wild thyme. Common woody shrubs include several species of heather, with their purple flowers, and gorse, which grows into large spiky bushes and can flower at any time of year,

Heading into woodland on the way to Ty'n-y-groes (Stage 2)

with small yellow flowers. Another species to look out for is bilberry, common on the descent from Y Garn on Stage 2A, which produces edible fruit in the autumn. Flower distribution in Snowdonia is governed by rock type, soil acidity, and other factors such as protection from grazing and availability of water. Some flowers are present in one valley but absent from the next for unknown reason; others such as the Snowdon lily are found nowhere else in the UK.

Away from the peaks, there are many woodlands in Snowdonia with a range of trees, mosses and ferns. The trees you are likely to see in conifer plantations are the larch and spruce, easily distinguished outside the summertime as the larch trees lose their needles in winter and the spruce do not. Up on the hills, there are many groups and scattered

individuals of birch, hawthorn and rowan, and even a few areas colonised by the locally rare juniper – one of only three native UK conifers alongside the Scots pine and the yew. It has been a project for the National Park to bring back this tree (mostly in shrub form in the mountains) to the hills of North Wales.

Away from the few trees and the heather, the hills are mainly grassy, with the dominant species being those which the sheep don't want to eat. These include matgrass, and in the damper places soft rush, purple moor grass and bog cotton, distinguished by its white tufted heads.

There are roughly 44 species of wild mammals in Snowdonia, and the lack of a precise number is due to the extremely rare nature of some species, which may well be locally extinct, such as the pine marten and

Hill ponies of the Carneddau

17

the red squirrel. Many mammals were hunted close to extinction by game-keepers and their numbers are low, although hopefully increasing since the persecution has largely stopped. These include polecat, fox, badger, otter, stoat and weasel. The wild mammals you are most likely to see are the American grey squirrel, and the wild ponies in the Carneddau. Of the smaller mammals, mice, voles and shrews can be found, and are quite common.

Of the large birds that live in the National Park, you're extremely likely to see ravens, buzzards and gulls. Of the smaller birds, listen out for the skylark and the stone chat when in the hills; they can often be heard but not seen. Meadow pipits and wrens are also common, and you may be lucky enough to see a chough, which is black with a red beak and legs and is more common in Snowdonia than the rest of the country. Look around in villages for the black-and-white pied wagtail – a small bird that is common around roads and buildings.

Another animal you're likely to encounter is the frog, which is ubiquitous in the hills; in the spring you'll find plenty of frogspawn in small pools or on the open grass where a damp spot used to be. There are also toads, alongside adders and the common lizard. There are many insects, from beetles to butterflies, and a range of lichen.

For a thorough guide to the wildlife you're likely to see, consider getting a copy of Mike Raine's book *Nature of Snowdonia*, which is an invaluable introduction to the area.

GEOLOGY

In order to understand where Snowdonia's mountains came from, we have to consider millions of years in which volcanoes, oceans, rivers and of course sheets of ice all played their part, and where the land was at times under the sea.

All of the rocks that make up Snowdonia are over 400 million years old, and those we see today were mainly laid down in three periods of geological time known consecutively as the Cambrian, the Ordovician and the Silurian. The work done to distinguish these periods, which are standard throughout the world, was actually carried out by geologists in Wales; the first period of 'Cambrian' is named after Wales itself, and the two periods of the Ordovician and Silurian were named after the pre-Roman Welsh tribes of the Ordovices and the Silures. In fact, much of the Ordovician tribe's land was in Snowdonia, so it's a nice tribute. The distinctions between the periods lie in the types of fossils found, as the Cambrian period is the first where substantial fossils were found, and where the first animals evolved.

The Cambrian period lasted from 541 to 485 million years ago and the rocks laid down are the oldest in Snowdonia, including a mix of igneous and sedimentary rocks. Today these can be found outcropping (on the surface) in a big central zone from the Mawddach estuary and Dolgellau to the Vale of Ffestiniog and Penrhyndeudraeth. Mountains made from Cambrian rock include the Rhinogydd and the hills east of Trawsfynydd. There is also an outcrop of Cambrian rocks running in a south-west to north-east line around Llanberis and Bethesda, which is where the rocks were laid down that would eventually become the slate that is so common in this area.

From 485 to 443 million years ago came the Ordovician period, where volcanic activity was intense, and where much of Snowdonia's current outcropping rock comes from. Ordovician rocks form the highest

The gorge from Pont Cae'n y Coed (Stage 2) – the rocks here are more than 500 million years old

peaks in a giant semicircle around the older Cambrian rocks in the heart of the Park. Snowdon, the Glyderau and the Carneddau are predominantly Ordovician, as is Cadair Idris much further south. Amongst the volcanic rock there are layers of sedimentary rock, and fossils have been found as high as the summit of Snowdon. It was during the Ordovician period that the first land plants evolved.

The later Silurian period, from 443 to 419 million years ago, doesn't play much of a role in our story because very few Silurian rocks remain within the National Park – the only ones on the route being to the north of Machynlleth. Outside the park they dominate, and if you travel south or east out of Snowdonia you are soon over Silurian rocks. There was less volcanic activity in this period, and the softer sedimentary rocks deposited were quickly eroded away by what happened next.

The next period, the Devonian, from 419 to 358 million years ago, saw a huge amount of pressure build up on the rocks of Snowdonia from the direction of the south-east. This pressure caused a rippling effect, pushing up a great mountain range that reached Himalayan height. The folds created during this massive uplift can still be seen in exposed mountainsides, and the highest part lay over the Rhynogydd, a formation known as the Harlech Dome.

There was then a period of hundreds of millions of years of erosion by water and ice, where the 8000-metre mountains were eroded down to about the height they are today. The upper Silurian rock, most recently deposited, was the first to be washed away, followed by the higher areas of Ordovician rock that formed the next layer down. This brings us roughly to what we see in the present. Silurian rock has gone from most of the Park, as has the Ordovician rock from the highest central area, exposing the Cambrian rock that forms the Rhynogydd and neighbouring hills. Snowdon and Cadair Idris are Ordovician mountains at opposite sides of what was the Harlech Dome, and the lonely survivors as their mountain parents were gradually washed into the sea.

It was the immense pressure of the Devonian that formed the slate that lies in several bands through the park. Originally laid down as mudstone or shale, these rocks were metamorphosed by such a high degree of pressure that their crystals realigned, allowing them to be split easily down one plane. These slate bands lie on either side of the Harlech Dome, at Llanberis, Bethesda and Blaenau Ffestiniog in the north, and around Corris and Abergynolwyn in the south.

Glaciation

Many ice ages have acted on Snowdonia over the years, and there have been as many as 20 in the last one and a half million years or so. The most recent ice age came to an end 10,000 years ago, and it is the action of the ice sheets and glaciers that resulted in many of the distinctive mountain features we see today.

Ice ages begin as, when the climate cools, snow begins to accumulate, and then doesn't melt in the summer. The places where these accumulations are most likely to happen are high in the mountains, in sheltered spots away from the sun. In the UK, with our prevailing weather from the south-west, this typically means the north-easterly, upper reaches of mountains. As the years pass the snow pack increases, until it eventually reaches a point where it is so heavy it begins to flow downhill, becoming a glacier. Ice sheets develop and glaciers merge and combine into great valley glaciers that flow out of the mountainous areas into the sea. Depending on the severity of the ice age, the sea itself may also be frozen.

The highest points of the glaciers, where they originate, are the great bowls gouged into the sides of many of our mountains. Known as cirques, they have the name *cwm* in Welsh, and are frequently the home of mountain lakes, formed when the gouging action of the glacier erodes down through the rock, or when rock-falls block the exits, preventing water from draining. Excellent examples can be seen at Llyn y Gadair on Cadair Idris, Cwm Llan on Snowdon and Cwm Idwal in the Glyderau.

Other classic glacial features are the arêtes (knife-edge ridges that form when two cirques nearly meet), U-shaped valleys such as the Nant Ffrancon where huge glaciers would have ploughed out the rock, and erratics, those odd boulders scattered haphazardly on fields and down valleys, which were carried there by the glaciers. You can also spot moraines – lines of debris, now covered in earth and vegetation, that mark the edges and end of the glacier, like the traces left by a bulldozer pushing aside a mound of earth.

It is important to realise that many ice ages have caused the mountains to look as they do, each one enlarging on the progress of the last. It is hard to work out exactly which features were caused by which ice age, but many features, such as the scratch marks left on the exposed bedrock by the glaciers, can only be dated to the last glaciation, which in the process wiped away the smaller features from before.

HISTORY

The earliest human structures found in Snowdonia date back to 2500BCE, a period when the climate was changing from warm and dry to colder and wetter. At that time, trees and scrub would have extended up to cover most of the mountains, and Neolithic settlements would have kept to the relatively clear coastal areas.

As the climate and human activity lowered the tree line, the introduction of livestock prevented trees from growing, and opened up the hills to larger flocks. Although not many of the settlements are left, there are plenty of remnants of life before the Roman

The Nant Ffrancon leading towards Bethesda – a U-shaped valley gouged out by glaciers (Stage 5)

Standing stones, Roman road and pylon at Bwlch y Ddeufaen (Stage 6A)

invasion to be found in the hills. There are chamber tombs, hill forts, stone circles and standing stones, and of course cairns – found almost everywhere including the summits – which are mostly Bronze Age burial chambers. There are also hut circles and burnt mounds, stacks of smashed rock and charcoal next to depressions where water would have been heated for cooking or leather tanning.

Alongside these common finds, there are large-scale workings such as the stone axe factory at Penmaenmawr and the copper mine on Great Orme, as well as well-preserved settlements and mines on the Llŷn Peninsula and Anglesey. The best place to see these remains on the route is on Stage 6 and 6A through the Carneddau. Further south, weapons have been found near

Beddgelert, and a magnificent bronze shield on Moel Siabod, which is now in the British Museum.

The Romans were attracted to North Wales by the deposits of copper and lead, and built a series of forts throughout the area. Roman roads can still be seen in the landscape, such as over the Bwlch y Ddeufaen in the Carneddau, and sections of track and embankment near Trawsfynydd. The Sarn Helen – the Roman road connecting North and South Wales – reached Segontium, present-day Caernarfon. It was the Romans who defeated the resident tribes, but during and after their occupation life went on as normal for most people, except of course for the persecution of the druids and the introduction of Christianity.

Snowdonia after the Romans left became part of the large but constantly changing kingdom of Gwynedd, ruled over by various princes and chieftains. In the late 12th century the Cistercians established their monastery at Cymer, and then from 1200 to 1240, Llewelyn the Great became Prince of Wales, with his power base coming from Gwynedd and the mountains of Snowdonia. Llewelyn was responsible for many of the Welsh castles in the area, including Castell y Bere, Dolwyddelan and Dolbadarn, and possibly a site on top of Dinas Emrys. There was a peace of sorts between an independent Wales and the English king, although Llewelyn the Great's grandson, Llewelyn ap Gruffudd (also called Llewelyn the Last), broke this peace during the reign of Edward I.

Edward retaliated by conquering Wales, converting it into an English colony in 1282. He was responsible for the huge castles that encircle the mountains at Conwy, Harlech and Caernarfon, and largely won by seizing the grain-producing island of Anglesey and starving out the Welsh. Edward I's son, Edward II, became the first English 'Prince of Wales' in a ceremony that took place in Caernarfon, starting a tradition that continues to this day for the heir to the throne.

Over 100 years later, beginning in 1400, Snowdonia featured in the 15-year revolt by Owain Glyndŵr against the English. He had parliaments at Dolgellau and Machynlleth, where he was declared Prince of Wales, and held several castles including Harlech. Intriguingly, his death was never recorded, and the myth endures that he disappeared into the mountains when the rebellion was over.

The atmospheric ruin of Llewellyn the Great's Dolwyddelan Castle (Stage 4)

23

After hundreds of years of war and rebellion, the first travellers began to arrive in Snowdonia gradually, since it was mostly seen as difficult to get to and hostile. The first 'modern' visits began in the 17th century, including by a number of botanists who made it to Snowdon and created important records of its flora. By the late 18th century the trickle had become a flood, and descriptions of 'tours' of this part of the world were widely published. The desire for tourists to visit Snowdonia, or 'The British Alps', increased during the Napoleonic Wars at the beginning of the 19th century when the traditional tour through Europe was impossible. This was the beginning of the immense popularity Snowdonia has experienced, drawing visitors for mountaineering, climbing,

hillwalking, touring and just enjoying the mountain scenery.

The last 200 years have seen the growth and decline of the slate industry, the continued presence of sheep farming and some cattle farming, and the growth of forestry. Other industries have come and gone. The general drive for people to have access to the mountains, and to conserve the landscape, gained huge momentum after World War II, and in 1949 an Act of Parliament was passed allowing the creation of National Parks. Snowdonia was one of the first three to be designated, in 1951, and it also contains many other layers of landscape protection, recognised by the UK government and the EU.

Today, tourism and outdoor activities are a major feature of life in the Park, where visitors enjoy the

The River Colwyn makes its peaceful progress through Beddgelert (Stage 4 and 4A)

mountains alongside their turbulent history, industrial past, and current farming and forestry.

UNDERSTANDING WELSH

You do not need to be in Wales for a long time to see that road signs, information boards and official documentation are bilingual. In the last census, around 20% of people living in Wales said they could speak Welsh, but in the county of Gwynedd, where the Snowdonia Way spends much of its time, this figure was above 60%. In some towns it is much higher.

Alongside the survival and growth of the Welsh language (Cymraeg), you'll see that most place names are in Welsh. The language hasn't changed much over the years, and it is still relatively easy to translate the meanings of place names. Throughout the text, I have tried to add the English translation of a place name in brackets after the Welsh name, which tells you something about the area. Many of the place names relate to times long past, and they are all to do with the landscape, famous inhabitants, religion or myth. Cymraeg is a language rooted in place and local identity, and understanding this will give you a greater insight into how the hills and villages got their names.

Hafod and Hendre

These two words are incorporated into some small place names – typically of farms and ruins. They relate to the practice of transhumance, where farmers used to spend the winter in the valley farm (*hendre*) before moving their whole families up with the flocks to the summer house in the hills (*hafod*). As the practice has died out, the husks of many former hafod buildings can be found in the hills. In recognition of this tradition, when the new café was opened on the summit of Snowdon in 2009, it was named Hafod Eryri ('Snowdonia summer house').

WHEN TO GO

Being on the west coast of Britain, Snowdonia has a mild climate, where rain can fall at all times of year. There is snow on the mountains frequently during the winter and sometimes down to the passes and valleys. Despite the stereotype that the UK's mountains are cold and wet, the spring, summer and autumn can be regularly warm and cloud-free. The low route of the Snowdonia Way is possible to walk all year round, although during very cold periods there can be snow on the passes. The high route stages are only possible in winter conditions with a full knowledge of winter mountaineering and appropriate equipment, including crampons and ice axe.

Mountain weather can change rapidly; low cloud, strong winds and heavy rain are possible at all times of year, but then again the risk of

Conwy and the Afon Conwy from one of the many towers in the town walls (Stage 6 and 6A)

sunburn is more common than you might think.

GETTING THERE

The whole route is served by several buses, and frequently encounters train lines. There are also plenty of taxi companies in and around the villages and towns. Remember that on Sundays and in the winter (November to Easter), most buses will operate a reduced service. The towns at the beginning and end of the route, Machynlleth and Conwy, both have railway stations. Public transport times can be looked up at www.traveline.cymru but the timings given on this site may not be 100% accurate so it may be worth calling the companies as well. See Appendix C for contact details of transport providers.

ACCOMMODATION

Places to stay are easy to find all along the route, ranging from campsites and hostels up to the very best hotels, and with everything in-between. Contact details for a selection of accommodation providers can be found in Appendix A. There are a few places where accommodation is sparse; where this is the case, details of nearby towns have been provided.

PLANNING YOUR ITINERARY

The low-level and high-level routes both run from south to north and include a number of places where you can combine or break up stages. The low route, as described in this guide, is walked in six days, but the following table includes an alternative itinerary of eight days for those who have more time and would like to cover the route at a more leisurely pace (including nights in Penrhyndeudraeth and Llanfairfechan during the longer stages of 3 and 6). The high route is walked in nine days. See Appendix B for tables of facilities available along both routes.

ROUTE DIFFICULTY

The main route, although low-level, varies between good tracks and indistinct paths, with everything in between. The trails can be uneven underfoot and the stages are full days of walking, typically with long stretches between shelter. Anyone of average fitness and stamina can complete the route – although the stronger your legs, the more you'll enjoy the uphills. To do this route, you should be comfortable walking for up to 8 hours per day in undulating terrain, carrying a pack.

The mountain route is, by definition, over the mountains, and is therefore much more challenging. Some of the stages are long and remote – especially Stage 6B – and you should have good fitness and stamina to attempt any of them. There are often sections of risk, close to steep drops and crags – most notably on Stages 1B, 4A and 5A. The paths are frequently obscure or non-existent, so good navigation is paramount. The ability to keep comfortable in changing weather, sometimes hours from shelter, is vital. To do this route, you should be comfortable walking for up to 10 hours per day over high peaks and moorland, with a suitable pack.

The Pyg Track (or Pig Track) on Snowdon (Stage 4A)

Six day low-level route		Eight day low-level route
Place	**Distance**	**Place**
Machynlleth	0	Machynlleth
Dolgellau	15½ miles (24.7km)	Dolgellau
Trawsfynydd	14 miles (22.6km)	Trawsfynydd
		Penrhyndeudraeth
Beddgelert	18½ miles (29.5km)	Beddgelert
Dolwyddelan	12¾ miles (20.6km)	Dolwyddelan
Bethesda	15½ miles (25.1km)	Bethesda
		Llanfairfechan
Conwy	21 miles (33.6km)	Conwy

WHAT TO TAKE

Mountain weather can change rapidly, and the temperatures and wind speeds on the walk, even when staying low, can be very different than in the villages and towns. Make sure you have warm clothes, waterproof jacket and trousers, food, water, walking boots, hat, gloves and scarf.

In addition, a good 'emergency' kit should include a first aid kit, head-torch and batteries, survival bag and whistle.

Take a charged mobile phone with you for emergencies. When choosing what clothes to walk in, opt for synthetic, wool or bamboo rather than cotton. (Cotton absorbs water, causing rubbing and making you colder.)

MAPS AND GPS

The maps in this book are extracts from OS 1:50,000 maps. Consider supplementing these with the 1:25,000 OS maps, which have greater detail and, crucially, show boundaries such as walls and fences. The maps that cover the whole route are:

- OS Explorer OL23 Cadair Idris & Llyn Tegid
- OS Explorer OL18 Harlech, Porthmadog & Y Bala
- OS Explorer OL17 Snowdon

For a wider perspective, the OS 1:50,000 maps that cover the route are:

- OS Landranger 135 Aberystwyth & Machynlleth
- OS Landranger 124 Porthmadog & Dolgellau
- OS Landranger 115 Snowdon/Yr Wyddfa

Distance	Nine day high-level route	
Distance	**Place**	**Distance**
0	Machynlleth	0
	Abergynolwyn	12 miles (19.5km)
15½ miles (24.7km)	Dolgellau	14¾ miles (23.6km)
14 miles (22.6km)	Trawsfynydd	16½ miles (26.6km)
9 miles (14.5km)	Penrhyndeudraeth	11¾ miles (18.9km)
9½ miles (15km)	Beddgelert	15¾ miles (25.2km)
	Pen y Pass	11¼ miles (17.9km)
12¾ miles (20.6km)		
	Capel Curig	9½ miles (15.5km)
15½ miles (25.1km)	Bethesda	12¾ miles (20.4km)
11¾ miles (19km)		
9¼ miles (14.6km)	Conwy	18 miles (28.7km)

Anyone walking any of the route stages described in this book should have a map and compass and know how to use them, or be with someone who can. A GPS is a useful addition to navigation, but should only come after map and compass proficiency. To this end the GPX files for the whole route are available as free downloads from www.cicerone.co.uk/856/GPX. They are useful for reassurance – especially over featureless terrain – but the whole route can be walked without ever needing a GPS.

Please take note that there are no waymarkers indicating the Snowdonia Way on the ground.

SAFETY

The main risks in the British mountains are slips and trips leading to injuries, and exposure to the elements leading to hypothermia (or at the opposite end, heat exhaustion). You should be ready to deal with these using the emergency kit recommended in 'What to take', but the next step after an incident should be to consider whether you should try to walk out, or whether you need to call Mountain Rescue.

If the risk is a loss of life or limb, always call Mountain Rescue, but in other situations remember that they may take several hours to reach you. If you need to call Mountain Rescue, dial 999, ask for 'Police', then 'Mountain Rescue'. If in doubt, always make the call; they will advise you of the best course of action over the phone. Have some basic information ready, such as your location and the nature of the incident.

Remember that Mountain Rescue members are all volunteers; if you love the mountains, please consider making a donation to the nearby team!

USING THIS GUIDE

At the start of every stage description is a box giving the day's vital statistics: start and end points, distance covered, total ascent, the time it's likely to take (not including rest or refreshment stops), the types of terrain you'll encounter, the height of the highest point en route (or, for the mountain route, the name and height of summits encountered), the OS sheet map required and any points at which supplies can be bought.

The route descriptions are an important addition to the stage maps. Where the route is not clear on the map there will be more detail, as maps simply can't show everything there is on the ground. Where a named feature is mentioned in the description that appears on the map, the first mention is shown in **bold** to help you keep track of where you are and so you can 'tick off' features as you see them.

Be aware that maps are never 100% accurate and route descriptions are only true at the time of writing. Things change. Fences are put up, forests cut down, and paths can become more/less distinct with time. Use your common sense. And remember, you're not lost; you're just taking the scenic route.

CLIMBING SNOWDON

As the highest mountain in Wales at 3560ft (1085m), Snowdon is a great hillwalking prospect for anyone doing the Snowdonia Way. It is climbed on the mountain route on Stage 4A and is begun from Beddgelert, meaning those on the main route can easily include Snowdon if they wish before returning to the low-level stages.

However, Stage 4A finishes in Pen y Pass – not somewhere the main route passes through. To get back onto the main route from here without doing the next mountain stage, main route walkers should spend the day after the Snowdon ascent walking from Pen y Pass to Dolwyddelan. This can be accomplished by following Stage 4B from Pen y Pass to the Bwlch y Rhediad and then Stage 4 from here to Dolwyddelan. This is a nice short day and walkers can then begin Stage 5 the next day.

Alternatively, you may wish to complete the whole of the main route to Conwy and then return to climb Snowdon afterwards. Public transport can easily be taken from Conwy to Bangor (train or bus) and then from Bangor to wherever you want to start the route from. Please check the transport map for guidance.

THE SNOWDONIA WAY

The waterfalls below Coed yr allt (Stage 4A)

STAGE 1
Machynlleth to Dolgellau

Start	Machynlleth town clock
End	Dolgellau town centre
Distance	15½ miles (24.7km)
Total ascent	2460ft (750m)
Time	7–8hr
Terrain	Track and minor road with some path sections; mostly dry and an easy gradient
Highest point	1335ft (407m)
Maps	OS Explorer OL23 Cadair Idris & Llyn Tegid
Supplies	Both Machynlleth and Dolgellau have a wide range of shops, cafés and pubs.

After leaving Machynlleth and crossing the Afon Dyfi, the route follows minor roads into the Dyfi Forest and the old slate mining region of Corris, where much of this history is still evident. Beyond Corris, the trail heads up a steep-sided valley to Aberllefenni and onwards above the village, following the Afon Llefenni into the hills.

The route leaves the forest paths to cross a high pass and head down into the valleys surrounding the mighty Cadair Idris. This great set of peaks watches over the landscape as the trail contours round its eastern side, following quiet lanes and heading through a peaceful natural woodland to drop down to Dolgellau.

The Afon Dyfi is in many minds the boundary between South and North Wales, and marks the southern boundary of Snowdonia west from here to the sea.

From the clock tower in the centre of **Machynlleth**, head north down the road Heol Pen Rallt. Follow the road as it swings left at the war memorial, signposted to the station. The road passes under a railway bridge and leaves the town.

Before the road crosses the bridge over the **Afon Dyfi**, turn right to follow the footpath next to the river. After a few hundred metres, cross the footbridge and head up the path to the main road. ◄

MACHYNLLETH ('THE PLAIN OF CYNLLAITH')

Nestling deep within the Dyffryn Dyfi (Dovey Valley), Machynlleth lies less than a kilometre away from the Afon Dyfi (River Dovey in English, but actually meaning 'dark river') and is surrounded by the hills and forests of Mid Wales. There is evidence of human activity dating back to the early Bronze Age, when copper mining took place in the surrounding area, and a standing stone, Maen Llwyd, can still be found in town dating from this period. The stone is now surrounded by a housing development and can be seen on the OS map in the south-east of town as 'standing stone'.

The Town Clock in Machynlleth

The Romans later occupied the area, building a fort at nearby Pennal. The most famous event in the town's history, however, took place in 1404, when Owain Glyndŵr was crowned Prince of Wales as part of his rebellion against the English, which had started in 1400. He also held his first parliament in Parliament House, which, although reconstructed in 1460, still stands on Maengwyn Street – the reason Machynlleth is also known as the 'ancient capital of Wales'. Parliament House now houses the Owain Glyndŵr Centre, which has an exhibition and is open to visitors from Easter to the end of September 10am–4pm and the rest of the year by arrangement (www.canolfanglyndwr.org, 01654 702932; call 01654 703336 to arrange out-of-season visits).A weekly market has been held in the town every Wednesday for over 700 years, since it received a market charter in 1291 from Edward I. Documents reveal that the market, and the two yearly fairs, attracted people from all over Wales and from over the border in England.

The nearby bridge over the Afon Dyfi has been there in some form since the 1500s, and the current bridge was built in 1805. It is the last bridge over the Dyfi before the sea, and has always been a site of strategic importance – so much so that there was a civil war skirmish nearby, where the Royalists holding the town were defeated by Cromwell's Roundheads in 1644. The

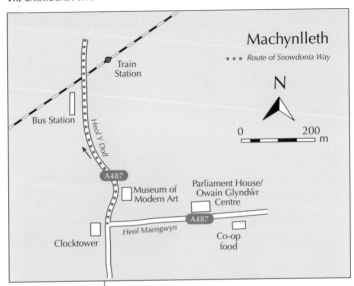

Machynlleth

••• *Route of Snowdonia Way*

N

0   200 m

Train Station

Bus Station

Heol Y Doll

A487

Museum of Modern Art

Parliament House/ Owain Glyndŵr Centre

A487

Heol Maengwyn

Clocktower

Co-op food

The first road bridge over the Dyfi

year before, Charles I had stayed in the town, in a house now called Royal House for this reason, and which also survives.

Further down the river where it meets the sea, the Dyfi Estuary is a designated UNESCO Biosphere Reserve due to its estuarine system and salt marsh habitat, and because of the native oak woodland further up the valley. Biosphere reserves are places where nature is conserved, and where communities are involved in sustainable development of the area.

The most conspicuous structure in town is the clock tower, at the main road junction in town. It was built in 1874 to celebrate the 21st birthday of Viscount Castlereagh, whose family lived in Plas Machynlleth, a large house on the edge of town. There are interpretation boards around the clock tower explaining the story of its construction.

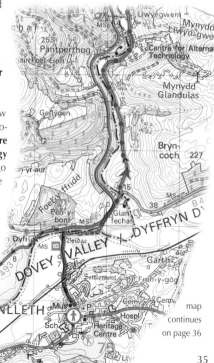

Go down the next road on the right, signposted to Llanwrin. After 100m the road crosses a bridge; after the bridge turn left onto the road signposted to the **Centre for Alternative Technology**.

Founded in 1973 to test new technologies for a more eco-friendly way of life, the **Centre for Alternative Technology** (CAT) is still the place to go to find out about renewable energy and sustainable living. You'll recognise the technology we now take for granted, such as wind turbines and solar panels, but alongside these well-known devices for energy production, CAT

map
continues
on page 36

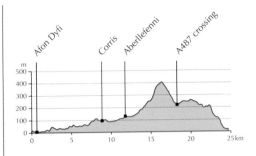

map continues on
page 39

has plenty of other methods to reduce your own environmental impact. Visitors can explore the gardens and displays, including a low-energy house and the water-powered railway. Open March to December every day 10am–5pm, and January to March for pre-booked groups only (www.cat.org.uk).

At the junction, where a road heads up towards the Centre entrance, continue straight on up a short section of track that soon rejoins the road. Follow the road onwards to **Esgairgeiliog Ceinws** (the first part of this name probably means 'ridge of Cyfeiliog').

Keep on the road through the village; when it leaves the village, follow it down to the bridge over the Afon Dulas. Turn right before the bridge and continue along the road to **Corris** ('little one'). The Dyfi forest is now on all sides.

Just before reaching the houses of Corris, take the path on

the right when the houses of the village become visible ahead. There is a wooden footpath post on the right of the road with a black metal rusted bench next to it. On the left is the entrance to Pentre Farm. Follow this path, and when it leaves the trees, Corris is visible on the left. The path forks just after passing a steep drop; take the left-hand fork, which goes downhill. The path now follows the **Afon Dulas** for a kilometre or so, where it joins a track next to some green huts.

Follow the track over the stream and then turn left at the T-junction. After crossing the bridge, turn immediately right onto a path. When this reaches a track, follow the uphill fork to the road at the entrance to **Aberllefenni** ('mouth of the river Llefenni'; *llefenni* means 'elm trees'). Turn right and head into the village.

SLATE MINING AT CORRIS AND ABERLLEFENNI

The slate industry in North Wales was a fundamental part of life for hundreds of years, and still shapes the landscape today. Slate was extracted both by quarrying, which is above ground, and mining, which was underground, and the terms are used interchangeably and sometimes inappropriately throughout Wales. Aberllefenni Slate Quarry, for example, is in fact a group of three mines, where most of the extraction was done underground.

The debris you see today are the spoil tips, where the waste slate was spilled out of the tunnels into the valley. The large cavernous opening visible on the other side of the valley from the route is Twll Golau, where the highest chambers of the Foel Grochan mine were joined up by mining out the intervening slate towards the end of the mine's life.

Slate mining here began in the 14th century, and the slate boom in the 19th century reached its peak in Aberllefenni in 1890 when 190 men were employed by the three mines. The slate here was of high quality and demanded a good price; this was the main reason why the mines were operated for so long. Despite fluctuations in their fortunes after the beginning of the 20th century and a decline to only employing 40 people after World War II, Aberllefenni only finally closed in 2003. At the time it was the longest continually operated slate mine in the world. Today, the slate mill still operates, working slate brought in from other mines and quarries in North Wales, and the spoil tips sit idly, becoming slowly inundated with vegetation.

The mines were serviced by a narrow gauge railway, which ran from the mines in the surrounding valleys down to Aberllefenni and Corris before heading to Machynlleth, where the slate could be loaded onto trains to the rest of Britain, or to the docks on the Dyfi at Derwenlas and Morben. Although most of it has been removed, some of the dismantled railway route can still be seen on the map, and a small section has been renewed from Corris to Maespoeth. The Corris Railway Museum is open to visitors, and rides can be taken on the trains on most weekend days throughout the summer (www.corris.co.uk).As can be seen on the surrounding hills, the land is now used extensively for plantation forestry. After World War I, the Forestry Commission began to afforest large parts of Britain, and the surrounding forests of Dyfi and Machynlleth cover nearly 60 square kilometres of hillside.

Follow the road past the slate workshop. Just past the red phone-box, bear left up the path towards the gate. There are some information boards and a large block of slate with 'Llwybr Yr Olwyn Wheel Walk' written on it in red glass beads. The route now heads into the Llefenni Valley.

Passing the spoil tips of the Aberllefenni slate quarries

The building on the right is the old quarry office, and the path now heads into the old slate quarry workings and spoil tips.

On the hillside to the right, when there is a view, you can see the vast entrance to the mine and the tips of slate spilling down to either side. This is a common sight in Snowdonia and understanding the history of slate mining is essential to understanding the history of the area.

map continues on page 41

Once past the spoil tips, the path drops down and meets a track beside some houses. Bear left on the track uphill. After 150m, before the track enters the forest, turn right down the steps following the footpath sign, and then left over the wall into the field.

Head across the field, keeping to its left, upper side along the fence. At the far side of the field, keep to the left of the upper wall corner and continue ahead, between the metal fence and the slate fence.

At the line of trees and small brook marking the end of this field, bear left up to a footbridge, cross it, and then turn immediately left up a short but steep slope. Head right after passing the wall and

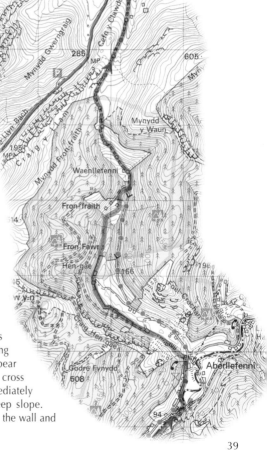

39

Following the path up the Llefenni Valley

continue on the path, which is again between a fence and a wall.

The distinct path leads to a set of wooden stables at **Hen-gae**. Pass through the yard and then bear left onto the footpath, which is signed. This footpath continues traversing the hillside for a kilometre and is mostly signed with yellow arrows, although sometimes the path can seem indistinct.

Pass through two kissing gates. At the first farm gate that the path comes to, go through it and continue ahead, soon bearing left uphill. At the next gate, the farm of **Fron-fraith** is visible to the left over fields. Go through this gate and continue ahead to another gate, which you also go through to reach a track. Walk along it for 60m until the fence on the right comes to an end. Follow the footpath arrows right off the track and then left, following a faint path over a fallen tree.

Cross the footbridge and head up the path to the road. Turn left onto the road going uphill, avoiding the farm track that is also on the left. The minor road is quite steep and heads right up over the pass ahead and down into the next valley. Soon after starting up it you finally enter the National Park, the boundary of which avoids the area around Corris because of the industrial landscape. From the top of the pass, the crags of Mynydd Ceiswyn can be seen on the right and the peak of Rhobell Fawr (big

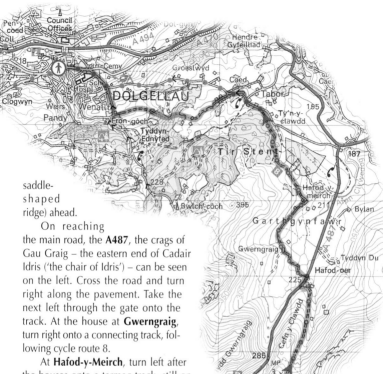

saddle-shaped ridge) ahead.

On reaching the main road, the **A487**, the crags of Gau Graig – the eastern end of Cadair Idris ('the chair of Idris') – can be seen on the left. Cross the road and turn right along the pavement. Take the next left through the gate onto the track. At the house at **Gwerngraig**, turn right onto a connecting track, following cycle route 8.

At **Hafod-y-Meirch**, turn left after the houses onto a tarmac track, still on route 8. Follow this track to a T-junction with the road. Turn left and follow the road; pass a turning on the right to **Tabor**, then the road swings left and goes downhill. Just after the first house on the left, turn left onto a track; there is a footpath sign pointing this way on the other side of the road.

The track soon bends right. At the fork soon after, bear right and follow the track between buildings and continue through the farm. At the fork where there are two gates, head through the right-hand gate into the field. Follow the faint track ahead through the field, keeping to the left side. Pass through a hole in the wall and ahead through a gate.

The path bends left through another gate. From here, head towards the ruined building ahead. After passing to

The path through the woods on the start of the descent to Dolgellau

the left of the ruined building, go straight ahead across the open field and at the far side, to the right of a house, turn right to follow a faint path. Soon a stile appears ahead, next to a gate on the left-hand side. Cross the stile and follow the path onwards.

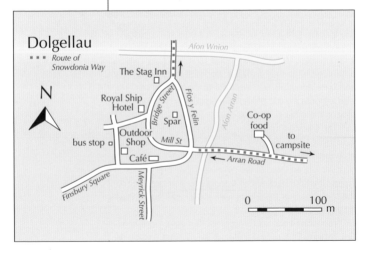

Dolgellau

▪ ▪ ▪ Route of
Snowdonia Way

N

Afon Wnion

The Stag Inn

Royal Ship
Hotel

Bridge Street

Ffos y Felin

Spar

Afon Arran

Co-op
food

to
campsite

bus stop

Outdoor
Shop

Mill St

Café

← Arran Road

Finsbury Square

Meyrick Street

0   100
▬▬▬▬▬▬ m

After 150m there is a faint path T-junction. Turn left, downhill through the trees. When this path reaches a wall with a house ahead over the field, turn left and follow the wall. Cross two stiles close together and then, after another 10 metres, bear left at the footpath sign, where the path is more distinct.

The path reaches a track next to some houses. Go ahead through the wooden gate onto the track to the left of the houses and follow it downhill. The northern crags of Cadair Idris are soon visible on the left, and Dolgellau appears ahead.

At the road, turn right. Turn left at the next two road T-junctions to arrive in **Dolgellau**.

DOLGELLAU

Nestled under the massive northern wall of Cadair Idris and sitting on the banks of the Afon Wnion (possibly 'white river'), Dolgellau ('meadow of monk's cells') is a market town in the heart of southern Snowdonia. The region was originally the land of the Ordovices, a Celtic tribe conquered by the Romans in 77–78CE, who built a fort nearby.

The town itself only came into existence in the 12th century as a serf village under the control of local chieftains, at a similar time to the founding of the nearby Cymer Abbey. It had become significant enough by the 15th century for Owain Glyndŵr to hold a parliament there in 1404 during his rebellion against the English. In 1657 the town received a visit from George Fox, who spread the seeds of Quakerism, which was to gain a key foothold in this part of Wales. The Quakers were persecuted by the established church, not willing to accept differences or challenges to its methods. This culminated in 1686, when the local farmer Rowland Ellis led an emigration to Pennsylvania in the United States.

Alongside leather tanning, the key industry in the town was woollen cloth, which thrived during the 18th century and was shipped to the world via the Mawddach Estuary, of which the Afon Wnion is a tributary. This declined during the 19th century due to mechanisation, to be replaced by the rise of the printing presses, which played a big role in the town from the construction of the first one in 1798.

The 19th century also saw several gold rushes in the area, the greatest of which began in 1887 and at its peak employed 500 men. Welsh gold is extremely rare and was expensive to extract; although most of the mines are now closed there is still some prospecting going on in the region.

Despite feeling remote, the town used to have a railway. The station has been completely obliterated, but the old line down the Mawddach Estuary is now a popular walking and cycling route. John Ruskin, famous inhabitant of the English Lake District, wrote that this was one of the finest walks he had ever done. It leads out above the great sands of the meandering river as it heads to the Irish sea near Barmouth, and is a great place to spot wildlife – particularly birds and flowers.

The descent into Dolgellau

STAGE 1A

Machynlleth to Abergynolwyn
(mountain route)

Start	Machynlleth town clock
End	Railway Inn, Abergynolwyn
Distance	12 miles (19.5km)
Total ascent	3575ft (1090m)
Time	6–7hr
Terrain	A mix of forest tracks and grassy paths, with some open hillside
Summits	Tarren Hendre (2077ft/633m)
Maps	OS Explorer OL23 Cadair Idris & Llyn Tegid
Supplies	Machynlleth has a wide range of shops; Abergynolwyn has a café and an inn.

The first section of this route leads out of Machynlleth and across the Afon Dyfi, following tracks through the southern end of the large Dyfi Forest before beginning the ascent up to Tarren Hendre, the most southerly 2000-foot mountain in Snowdonia. After reaching the summit of Tarren Hendre, the path leads down into another large conifer forest where the old slate quarry workings of Bryn Eglwys are partially hidden by the vegetation. The final descent runs along the stream-side of the Nant Gwernol through a beautiful patch of woodland down to Abergynolwyn.

From the clock tower in the centre of **Machynlleth**, head north down the road Heol Pen Rallt. Follow the road as it swings left at the war memorial, signposted to the station. The road passes under a railway bridge and leaves the town.

Cross the bridge over the Afon Dyfi and turn left after the bridge along the road, then take the first road on the right, steeply uphill, which is marked as a dead end. Continue up this road until a footpath sign with a yellow man on it points to a faint path on the left, through a gate. Follow this path diagonally uphill over the grassy hillside, keeping the woodland and the dense bracken on the left. Soon you will see some white-topped posts you can follow through this field, and before long you will see a conifer forest ahead.

The path bears right, so the conifer forest is soon on the left as the path heads steeply uphill, reaching the hill crest. There is a stile in the corner of the field next to the top of the forest. Cross it and head straight downhill, following the path.

Turn left on the major forest track, and at the first fork, stay right, following cycle route 8 and footpath signs. Follow the track downhill for a while until reaching the road north of **Pennal** (either 'head of the moor' or 'region of the enemy'). There is a track junction before this road at which you should continue straight ahead. The road itself is tarmac. Turn left and follow the road to the next junction, then turn right.

map continues on page 49

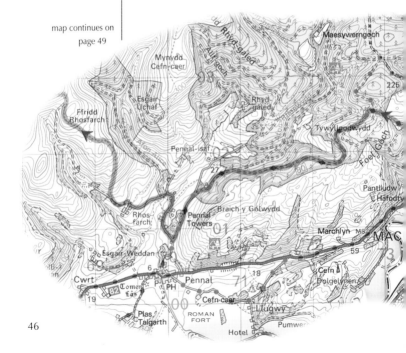

The road crosses the river Afon Rhonwydd and bends left. At the fork immediately after the bend, go left onto the track. This track crosses another stream, the **Afon Alice**, and then bends right; at this point continue straight ahead onto a joining track. This track heads uphill and approaches the farmhouse of **Rhos-farch**. Take the track on the right, which aims to the right of the house.

At the house, turn right up to a set of two gates next to each other. Go through the left gate and follow the track ahead, which soon bends left as it heads uphill.

The track bends right again as it heads into a valley. After 200m, turn right, uphill, following another track at the Y-junction. This track is less distinct than the one you are on so look out for it.

The track is steep at first and bends right, then becomes less clear as it levels out and bends left, keeping to the right of a summit knoll. As the path bends left after passing the summit, it reaches two gates 20m apart. Go through the left gate and follow the fence ahead. The fence heads north-west to pass to the left side of the next peak, the high point of **Fridd Rhosfarch**.

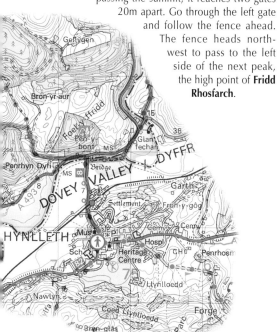

47

After the farm at Rhos-farch, take the track on the right

A **'fridd'** is an upland enclosure used for the farming of mountain sheep. It is large but enclosed either by a fence or a wall, and is used for keeping sheep at certain times of year, when otherwise they roam free on the mountain.

The path swings back right as it passes this peak and reaches a stile over a wall. Cross the stile and head up the steep slope of **Tarren Rhosfarch** ahead, where there is a winding path.

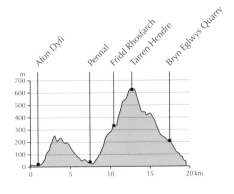

48

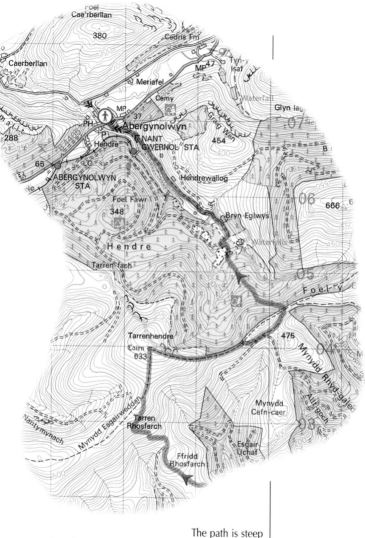

The path is steep up to the ridge of **Mynydd Esgairweddan**. Once on the ridge you will come to a fence, which runs along it. Leave the path and turn right along the fence, following

Looking back at Tarren Hendre from the ridge

it to the top of **Tarren Hendre** (*tarren* means 'escarpment' and *hendre* means 'winter house').

Tarren Hendre is a grassy peak and part of a long ridge of hills running east-west above the Dyfi. The mountains of Mid Wales are all laid out to the south of this high but rounded hill – including Plynlimon, the source of the River Severn and the River Wye – and the Dyfi estuary leads west to the sea.

From the summit, follow the east ridge down; there is also a fence running down this ridge but make sure you have the right one. The path becomes distinct and leads down to a low point between Tarren Hendre and a small peak on the same ridge.

Follow the grassy ridge path as it bends right to skirt this peak. The path descends to meet a track. Once on the track, go ahead for 40m and then turn left onto the path that leads up to the col, where a wooden post is visible, to the north-west of the peak at 475m. The junction for this path is not obvious from the track.

On the col, continue following the path, which bears left, traversing the slope to rejoin the main ridge at the corner of a fence. Tarren y Gesail is visible dominating the skyline ahead. At the fence corner, turn left off the ridge onto a faint path towards the forest of Hendre. After 10m cross the stile and then follow the path as it swings left. The path becomes clear when you enter the forest and descends diagonally downhill.

At the large forestry track, continue straight ahead over it onto the path that continues downhill. The path can be muddy, but follow it straight down. When it emerges from the forest, the quarry workings of **Bryn Eglwys** are visible ahead.

ABERGYNOLWYN AND BRYN EGLWYS SLATE QUARRY

The exposed slate in the upper valley of the Nant Gwernol began to be exploited in the 1840s, becoming Bryn Eglwys quarry. Production increased in 1864 with the formation of the Aberdovey Slate Company Limited, and at a similar time, the village of Abergynolwyn ('mouth of the river Gynolwyn') was built to house the mineworkers and their families. At its peak the quarry employed 300 men.

Due to the relative isolation of the quarry, the slate proved difficult to get to local transport links south in the Dyfi Valley. The Company built the Talyllyn railway to take the slate west instead, down to Twywn on the coast, where it could be packed onto ships or onto the main Cambrian railway. A tramway used to run all the way up to the quarry, but the restored Talyllyn railway now stops at Nant Gwernol, in the trees just above Abergynolwyn. It now carries passengers on trips up and down the line and is open from late March to October (www.talyllyn.co.uk). Every August hundreds of people take part in racing the train from Twywn to Abergynolwyn and back, a race organised by the local rotary club; about 10% of the runners succeed.

Despite brief closure from 1909 to 1911, the quarry kept operating until a major collapse caused it to finally close in 1946, roughly 100 years after slate was first extracted on the site. Today there are paths where walkers can view the old quarry pits, which are being colonised by the adjacent woodland. The local area and the village now occupy themselves with forestry, farming and tourism.

The path bears right to pass quarry workings, heading into the valley. When the path reaches a stony track, turn

Abergynolwyn, the old slate mining village where the Nant Gwernol meets the Afon Dysynni

To explore more of the slate works, turn left here to find a trail with a few information boards.

right. ◀ After 100m, the track bends left and becomes a path. Follow the path through woodland past mine tips and shafts. When it reaches a crossroads of tracks, continue straight on, then after 200m turn left at the signpost to the station. Go through a kissing gate onto a path downhill into the woodland of Coed Hendrewallog and Coed Nant Gwernol. At the fork halfway down, go left down the stony path.

Follow the path down to the **Nant Gwernol** ('alder stream') and along it; do not cross the first bridge, and keep to the right of the stream. Later on, when the path forks just above the bridge to the station, take the left fork but do not cross the bridge, keeping to the path on the right of the stream. When this joins a minor road, turn left to descend to **Abergynolwyn** and shortly arrive at the village centre and car park, with The Railway Inn opposite.

STAGE 1B

Abergynolwyn to Dolgellau
(mountain route)

Start	Main car park next to community centre, Abergynolwyn
End	Dolgellau town centre
Distance	14¾ miles (23.6km)
Total ascent	4890ft (1490m)
Time	8hr
Terrain	Upland grassy tracks with some sections of path; faint paths on the descent of Cadair Idris finishing with minor road into Dolgellau
Summits	Cadair Idris (2930ft/893m)
Maps	OS Explorer OL23 Cadair Idris & Llyn Tegid
Supplies	Abergynolwyn has a café and an inn; Dolgellau has a wide range of shops.

The finest mountain walk in south Snowdonia, the traverse of Cadair Idris is a proper adventure. Starting in the quiet village of Abergynolwyn and taking tracks through the upper reaches of the Dyffryn Dysynni, the trail passes the atmospheric ruin of Llewellyn the Great's famous Castell y Bere before gaining height towards Cadair Idris. This large atmospheric valley is not as well visited as the popular routes further east, and you will probably only be sharing it with the sheep and the birds.

On reaching the main ridge, the traverse begins, leading east to the summit at Penygadair along rocky paths, with cliffs falling away dramatically to the north. A wide track then leads along the ridge to Mynydd Moel, where there is plenty of time to enjoy the views on all sides. At the far end the route descends the wild and wide ridge of Gau Graig, finally turning north through woodland to reach Dolgellau.

From the car park in the centre of **Abergynolwyn**, go left down the main road past the Railway Inn. Turn right down the track after the playground, which runs along the Afon Dysynni ('boundary river'). Cross the river at the footbridge on the left and follow the path ahead.

Following the Afon Dysynni away from Abergynolwyn

The path bends right at the house, enters a field and disappears. Continue in the same direction across the field and the path soon reappears. It ascends slightly and traverses the hillside above the **Afon Dysynni**. At the fork after 1km, go right, downhill towards the river.

When the path reaches the road at **Pont Ystumanner**, turn right to cross

map continues on page 56

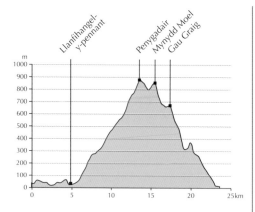

the bridge and follow the road to the road junction with the phone-box. Turn right and head towards the farm at **Caerberllan**. Continue past the farm gates and go through the next gate on the left, 100m further on.

Follow the track up into a field, where it disappears. Continue straight ahead across the field and through scattered trees, keeping at the same height. A faint path is sometimes visible, and there is a fence on the left.

Once across the field, there is a grassy track and then a set of two gates in parallel fences. Go through both gates and continue ahead on the track. **Castell y Bere** is visible on its prominent rock ahead. Stay on the track until it reaches a metal corrugated iron shed and a private sign on a gate.

CASTELL Y BERE

Rising out of a rocky outcrop at the heart of the Dysynni Valley stand the ruins of Castell y Bere, which seems to grow from the rock itself. Built in the early 1220s by Llewelyn the Great, it was one of the first stone castles built by the Welsh Princes, placed to defend the princedom of Gwynedd and guard Llewelyn's cattle, which were vital to the local population.

The castle was occupied by the Welsh for over 60 years, finally being lost to Edward I by Llewelyn the Great's grandson Llewelyn ap Gruffudd. Edward made modifications to the castle and even tried to start an English town in the surrounding valley. These efforts proved unsuccessful, however, and the castle was finally abandoned in 1294 after a Welsh uprising, during which the castle was possibly taken by the Welsh and burnt down.

The remnants you see today, which are managed by Cadw (cadw.gov. wales), are free to explore; as a fortification it is hugely impressive and the position provides great views down the Dysynni Valley and up towards Cadair Idris.

To visit Castell y Bere, turn left on the road where the route reaches Llanfihangel-y-pennant.

On the left is a stile. Cross it and follow the fence down and then right, to the corner where it turns right again uphill. Rather than following the white arrows, look left at the telegraph pole halfway down the sloping field. There are yellow footpath arrows on it. Go straight downhill past the pole and cross the stream at the footbridge.

Cross the stile ahead and turn right on the road in **Llanfihangel-y-pennant** (a left turn here would take you to Castell y Bere); continue along the road to **Tynyfach** and cross the bridge. Follow the road as it bends right after the bridge, passing **Tyn-y-ddôl**, the home of Mary Jones.

This ruin and monument mark the site of the house of **Mary Jones**, who became famous for walking 25 miles barefoot from here to Bala to purchase a Welsh bible in 1800. Thomas Charles, the clergyman who she bought the bible from, was inspired by the event, and the relative scarcity of bibles in Wales, to set up the Bible Society. The Society's mission is to make the Bible available throughout the world, and it is amazing to think that this global effort traces back in part to this small cottage in the Welsh hills.

Follow the road until it becomes a track at **Gwastadfryn** and continue following it uphill. After just over 2km, at the sheep pens at **Hafotty Gwastadfryn**, cross the stream to the pens and go ahead, bearing slightly right to cross the stile at the gate with the blue arrow marker on a yellow background. Continue along the track ahead.

The track soon feels more like a path. At a fork, keep right to pass through a gate, then follow the path as it bends to the right. This path, the Rhiw Gwredydd, takes you up to the ridge of **Cadair Idris**, roughly 2km further on. ▶

The point at which the path meets the ridge gives spectacular views north to the Rhinogs and the rest of Snowdonia.

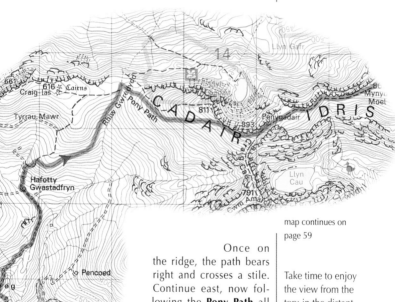

map continues on page 59

Once on the ridge, the path bears right and crosses a stile. Continue east, now following the **Pony Path** all the way to the highest point of Cadair Idris at **Penygadair** ('top of the chair'). The path has some rock steps but is mostly very loose stones. ▶

Take time to enjoy the view from the top; in the distant north Snowdon is visible, with the Glyderau and then the Carneddau to its right.

57

Heading up to Cadair Idris

CADAIR IDRIS

The massive ridge of Cadair Idris, with its spectacular north-facing cliffs and its several glacial lakes, is the southern extent of the Ordovician rock pushed up during the creation of the Harlech Dome. It is the same age as the rocks that form Snowdon, and all the hills that lie between them are older, dating to the Cambrian period. If you can see from the summit to Snowdon, try to imagine millions of years into the past, where the mountains here rose to 8000 metres.

The name means the 'chair of Idris', who was either a mythical giant who used the mountain as a literal seat, or a local chieftain whose lands were nearby. The most famous myth associated with Cadair Idris is to do with the bardic tradition of sleeping alone on the summit: morning would find you either dead, mad, or a poet. This myth has also been associated with Snowdon, but it's certainly worth giving it a go if you have the time.

From the summit, continue east along the ridge to the peak of **Mynydd Moel** via a wide grassy path. After this point the ridge turns south-east and descends steeply. After this descent, cross the stile and then stay on the left of the fence that runs along the ridge. Follow the fence as the ridge bends north-east. After passing the high point at 683, begin the descent of **Gau Graig**.

Cross the stile over the first fence you come to, then cross the stile at the wall junction further down to continue along the ridge path. The descent is mostly on a grassy path, although there are a few rocky steps.

After a while, a wall appears ahead angled diagonally across the ridge. Cross the stile that leads to the right-hand side of the wall (SH 750 149). If you go too far a wall junction is reached with no way ahead, so simply follow the right-hand wall back up for 30m or so to find the stile.

Now on the right of the wall, continue descending. The path follows the wall, then bears right, away from the wall. Follow it down to cross a stile. Descend straight down and pass through gaps in two parallel fences only 20m apart. About 30m after this there are two parallel ruined walls.

59

Turn left to follow the first wall. Keep the wall on the right and a distinct path soon appears, with yellow footpath arrows. Follow the path uphill, avoiding following the wall as it bends right towards a knoll. Towards the top of the crest the path pretty much vanishes but just go straight on over the top if in doubt, heading north-west towards Bwlch-côch.

Once over the top, bear slightly left and head downhill between fences towards a wall, where there is a gate and a stile. Descend through the next field, and at the bottom go through the hole in the wall on the right-hand side, then keep going downhill on the path, with a ruined wall on your left.

Pass the barn and follow the path, which turns left and then reaches sheep pens at **Bwlch-côch**. Cross the stile to the right of the pens and continue 50m along a track to the next gate and the start of a minor road. Go ahead down the road, turning right at the T-junction in the woods, left at the next road T-junction and then left at the third T-junction to arrive in **Dolgellau**.

Dolgellau from Cadair Idris

STAGE 2
Dolgellau to Trawsfynydd

Start	Bridge over Afon Wnion, Dolgellau
End	Cross Foxes Inn, Trawsfynydd
Distance	14 miles (22.6km)
Total ascent	2590ft (790m)
Time	7hr
Terrain	Paths for the first section, some faint. Tracks for most of the route through Coed y Brenin and then faint paths again to finish through farmland
Highest point	1178ft (359m)
Maps	OS Explorer OL18 Harlech, Porthmadog & Y Bala
Supplies	Dolgellau has a wide range of shops; Coed y Brenin visitor centre has a cafe; Trawsfynydd has small shops and an inn.

Mostly a day of vast forest, the route begins with a path that traverses the hillside on the western side of the Afon Mawddach through broadleaved woodland and open slope. After entering the forest of Coed y Brenin, easy tracks lead north, where breaks in the trees give views over to the hills of the Rhinogs. As the route heads through the forest, there are hidden glimpses both of the area's medieval iron-working past, and its origins as a volcanic landscape.

Leaving Coed y Brenin, the trail leads over the open moorland characteristic of the east of Snowdonia, before descending towards Trawsfynydd through farmland. For much of this final section the great Llyn Trawsfynydd is visible next to the town, before the land drops away in the north to the Vale of Ffestiniog.

From **Dolgellau**, cross the Afon Wnion via the main road bridge and turn left onto the road at the T-junction. Turn right up the next road, Pen Y Cefn Road, signposted to the golf course. Continue up this road, which is quite steep. At the top of the road, as it turns right, turn left towards the golf club.

Follow the road to the right of the golf club car park and continue ahead along the track towards the gate. Ignore the track on the right, which leads onto the golf course. Once through the gate, continue ahead down the path, with Y Garn now visible in front of you. At the road, go straight ahead, passing the bollards onto the old bridge over the **Afon Mawddach** ('little Mawdd river'). ◄

Turn right down the track before the river crossing to visit nearby Cymer Abbey.

map continues on page 64

Cymer Abbey is a Cistercian Abbey built in 1198–99 under the patronage of Maredudd ap Cynan, Lord of Merionnydd. The Cistercian Order spread throughout Europe in the Middle Ages and was known for its austerity and practice of manual labour. The abbeys were built away from towns in sites of seclusion, which explains the large numbers in Wales and northern England. Cymer Abbey was relatively poor, despite being near the lowest ford on the Afon Mawddach, and was already in a state of decline when it was dissolved by Henry VIII in 1536–7. It is open to visitors 10am–5pm April to October and 10am–4pm November to March. Entry is free.

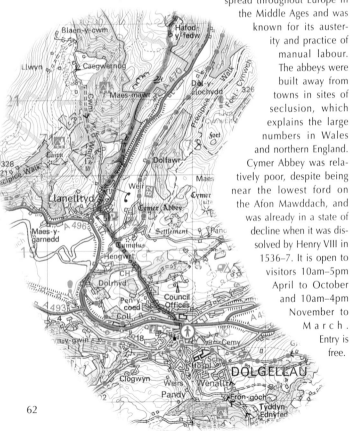

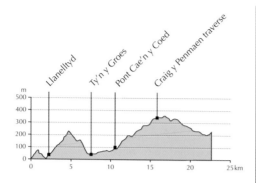

Beyond the bridge, turn immediately right onto the footpath, following it straight over the next track junction to reach **Llanelltyd** ('church of St Elltud'). Cross the main road and go up the steps, following the footpath sign. Turn right at the next junction.

At the road T-junction, turn left and then almost immediately right onto a footpath into the woods, which is signposted. Follow this path through the woods, ignoring faint side paths. At the stile before a path crossroads, continue ahead. When the path leaves the trees, the view opens out down to the river and across to the hill of Foel Cynwch.

The path continues its traverse halfway up the hillside, below the crags of **Maes-mawr**, now on an open hillside. Upon reaching a wall, go through the gate into the woodland ahead. The path continues ahead, and becomes less clear when it leaves the woods. There are small rocky outcrops on the right-hand side and the path soon reaches a wide circular ruined wall.

Go straight ahead across the circle and then turn right towards the buildings that come into view not far away. Keep to the right of the buildings, and turn left immediately after them. Go straight ahead. The path is soon more distinct, eventually becoming a track, entering the woods and going downhill. There is a footpath sign on a tree at the entrance to these woods.

The track winds downhill and crosses a stream, bearing right on the other side. Follow the track until it reaches two stone buildings. Go through the gate and pass the buildings, shortly reaching a track junction, where you will see a footpath post on the right. Ignore this post and turn left, through the gate, to a track going uphill. Leave the track after 50m and pass through the gate ahead, following a grassy trail which soon turns right over the stream.

map continues on page 67

After this stream the path is indistinct, but bear to the right, around the hillside, keeping at the same height; a house will soon appear ahead. Pass to the left of the house, and immediately after the garden wall ends, turn right downhill and then almost immediately left onto the path. Go through the metal gate, cross the bridge over the stream and continue ahead along the faint path through the woods.

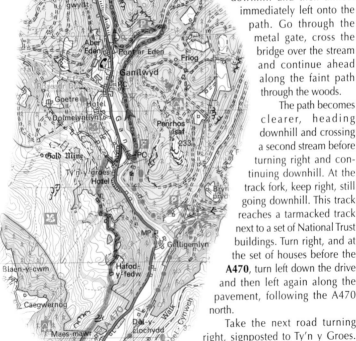

The path becomes clearer, heading downhill and crossing a second stream before turning right and continuing downhill. At the track fork, keep right, still going downhill. This track reaches a tarmacked track next to a set of National Trust buildings. Turn right, and at the set of houses before the **A470**, turn left down the drive and then left again along the pavement, following the A470 north.

Take the next road turning right, signposted to Ty'n y Groes.

The Rhinogs from Coed y Brenin

Follow this road across the bridge to the **car park**. ▶ Go past the toilet block to the T-junction and turn left onto the track, which at first goes gently uphill past the car park. Soon on the left you can look up at the impressive Craig-y-cae crags on the slopes of Y Garn.

If you have time there is an impressive stand of Douglas Firs a short walk to your right, some of which are named!

You are now in **Coed y Brenin** ('woodland of the king'), which in the 1990s began its transformation from a plantation forest into the mountain biking and trail running centre it is today.

The track bends right after passing houses and fields on the left and the village of **Ganllwyd** on the far side of the river. The track enters the forest, and you reach Pont Cae'n y Coed, the first bridge you come to, above a deep gorge. Turn left off the track to cross the bridge. Pass through the **car park** onto the road and continue ahead along it.

Shortly, when the road bends to the left, turn right onto a track. This is a wide forest track built to take vehicles; ignore the smaller cycle paths or you run the gauntlet of the mountain bikers! This track stays roughly level as it bends right around the hillside. At the junction, turn right along the tarmacked track, gently uphill. When this track forks, take the right fork uphill.

This track passes a stone wall and fields on the right. Continue ahead, where a footpath sign appears announcing the track as 'Council Road'. At the major track junction when the fields on the right come to an end, continue ahead along the track uphill, still on Council Road. ◀

If you turn left here, you can descend to a visitor centre and café.

At the next junction when the track bears right, continue ahead at another Council Road sign. Views to the Rhinogs soon open out on the left and you can see Rhinog Fawr, from this angle a triangular peak. Follow another Council Road sign ahead and pass the sign for the bloomeries – former charcoal-making and iron-smelting sites whose ruins are worth a visit.

The Rhinogs come into view again on the left when you reach a small set of fields. At the crossroads, go ahead uphill, not following Council Road. At the track junction, turn right. ◀ You can see the crags of Craig y Penmaen ahead. Take another right turn soon after at the next junction; the track climbs and bends left, beginning the traverse beneath **Craig y Penmaen**. Scattered around this area – and perhaps forming this very track – are remnants of the ancient trail of the Sarn Helen.

Stage 2A joins the route here.

Running 160 miles from North to South Wales is the Roman road of **Sarn Helen** (actually Sarn Elen, meaning 'road of the legion'), built to link up the various forts and settlements the Romans constructed as part of their occupation of Wales. Although much of the route is invisible today, or has been built over by modern roads, some sections remain, including on the hillside north of Coed y Brenin. This section would have linked the fort of Tomen-y-Mur to the north of Trawsfynydd with the fort near Dolgellau. Imagine doing today's walk in full armour and carrying a shield, and maybe your backpack won't seem so heavy!

map opposite continues on page 69

When fully out of the forest you will be able to see the full day's route laid out before you, from Cadair Idris in the south to Llyn Trawsfynydd ahead. Continue ahead along the track, passing Craig y Penmaen and following a wall on the right. Take the right track at the fork, heading uphill, rather than the grassy left one heading downhill.

The track meets the road beside a small forest and the chapel Capel yr Annibynwyr Penystryt, built in 1890. Turn left on the road and then left at the road junction. Cross the cattle grid and take the right road fork, passing to the right of the house.

This minor road gradually descends, and from the small group of conifers you can see Llyn Trawsfynydd ahead. Continue down the road for just over 1km to **Tyddyn Bach** farm; turn right and walk up the farm drive, where there is

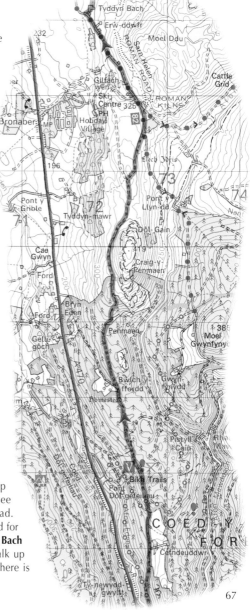

67

a footpath sign on a metal post. Go ahead through two gates, following the track into a small concrete yard. Here there are several gates; go through the one straight ahead, between the wooden telegraph pole and the small stone barn.

Immediately turn left and follow the fence, through a gate and ahead across the field beyond, keeping to the left. On the far side of the field, a stone slab acts as a bridge over the stream and there is a stile with a footpath sign. Continue ahead across the next field, keeping the wall on your left.

Go through the gate on the left of the house into the enclosure, where there are several trees. Exit the enclosure via a small gate on the far side, onto a gravel track. Turn right towards the farm, then left when the track forks, between the barns and through the black gate ahead. Cross the stream and turn immediately left at the footpath sign through the field, keeping away from the marshy area nearer the stream.

Halfway across the field you pick up a ruined wall, which acts like a raised embankment; follow it. Go through a gap in the fence and follow the wall on your left as it goes gently downhill. At the bottom corner of

Llyn Trawsfynydd comes into view

the field, cross the stile on the left and go straight ahead, crossing another stile and then over a wall via stone steps.

Turn right and follow the wall. On the horizon you can see Moelwyn Mawr ('great white hill') and the surrounding peaks. After the wall bends right, cross the stile and cross the grass to the track in front of the farm buildings at **Plâs Capten**. Turn left on the track and follow it to the road. Turn left on the road and head downhill to the A470. Cross here and head up the opposite road, reaching the high street of **Trawsfynydd**. Continue up the high street and pass the village shop to reach the Cross Foxes Inn.

TRAWSFYNYDD

Meaning 'across the mountain' Trawsfynydd is mostly known for its large artificial lake and the adjacent nuclear power station, which can be seen from the summits of all the nearby mountains. The area was inhabited during the Bronze Age and then by the Romans who built the fort and amphitheatre at Tomen y Mur on the hillside above the town. The Normans later built a castle on the same site, and although not much is left today the outlines and embankments of the buildings are clearly visible on the land.

The lake was created in 1924–28 with several dams and the diversion of the Afon Prysor ('river of the heap of brushwood'), the main river feeding the lake from the east. Its original purpose was to power the Maentwrog hydroelectric power station in the valley to the north, which used to be able

The statue of Hedd Wyn

to provide electricity for the whole of North Wales. The nuclear power station was built in 1959, a controversial decision since the National Park had already been designated. It used the lake water for cooling, and because of this essential resource, the hydro-electric scheme was limited to using just the top few feet of water.

In the centre of the village is the statue of Hedd Wyn, a Welsh bard who among other subjects wrote about the young men of the area who had gone to fight at the start of World War I. He later joined up, and was killed in Flanders in 1917, shortly before being awarded the winning prize in that year's National Eisteddfod for his poem 'The Hero'.

The late 19th century saw Trawsfynydd linked to Bala by a railway line running over 30 miles through the mountains. The line was later dismantled, and today Trawsfynydd has a remote and wild feel, sitting as it does high above the Vale of Ffestiniog in the vast central hills of North Wales. The nuclear power station and the railway that served it have been decommissioned. The lake is popular for fishing and a path running around it has been built with EU funding to bring walkers and cyclists to the area.

STAGE 2A

Dolgellau to Trawsfynydd
(mountain route)

Start	Bridge over Afon Wnion, Dolgellau
End	Cross Foxes Inn, Trawsfynydd
Distance	16½ miles (26.6km)
Total ascent	4560ft (1390m)
Time	9hr
Terrain	Faint paths and open rough mountainside for the first half of the day; after passing Craig Aberserw there are wide tracks, minor roads and farmland paths
Summits	Y Garn (2064ft/629m)
Maps	OS Explorer OL18 Harlech, Porthmadog & Y Bala
Supplies	Dolgellau has a wide range of shops; Trawsfynydd has small shops and an inn.

Heading out of Dolgellau, the route climbs quickly to the New Precipice Walk and the spectacular views down the Mawddach Estuary to the Irish Sea. Mountain paths then lead up the wide and grassy south ridge of Y Garn to its summit, and then down the far side, where a pathless route leads through a hillside of heather and bilberries into and across the wild valley beyond. After miles of remote moorland, with the Rhinog mountains towering above you in the west, an easy track is finally found to lead you towards the forest of Coed y Brenin.

After a brief ascent through the northern edge of the forest, the route passes under the crags of Craig-y-Penmaen before leading down to Trawsfynydd through farmland. Ahead at this point is the impressive Llyn Trawsfynydd, with the Moelwyn mountains beyond.

From **Dolgellau**, cross the Afon Wnion via the main road bridge and turn left onto the road at the T-junction. Turn right up the next road, Pen Y Cefn Road, signposted to the golf course. Continue up this road, which is quite steep. At the top of the road, as it turns right, turn left towards the golf club.

Follow the road to the right of the golf club car park and continue ahead along the track towards the gate. Ignore the track on the right, which leads onto the golf course. Once past the gate, continue ahead down the path, with Y Garn now visible in front of you. At the road, go straight ahead, passing the bollards onto the old bridge over the **Afon Mawddach** ('little Mawdd river').

After crossing the bridge continue ahead up the path to the left of the small building towards **Llanelltyd** ('church of St Elltud'). Cross over the main road towards the bollards, pass between them, and bear left along the minor road.

Follow the road over the bridge. The road then bears right; follow it until the point where it nearly rejoins the main road. On the right, there is a footpath going uphill, beginning with three steps and signposted towards the 'New Precipice Walk'. Follow this path up into the forest.

map continues on page 75

At the first path fork, take the left route uphill, rather than the one that follows the wall. The path crosses a fence at a stile; go ahead and after 30m two paths appear on the right. Take

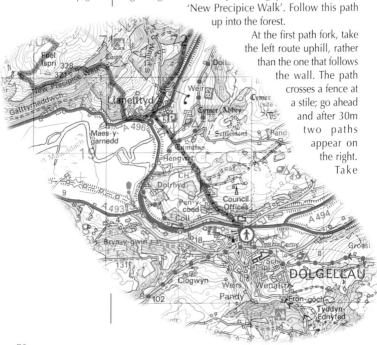

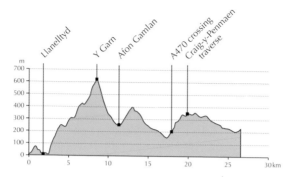

the one that goes uphill. Shortly you will reach another fork; bear left and cross the wall over a stile. A lake – Llyn Tan-y-graig – will soon appear on the right.

The path soon bends right and goes uphill between trees. At the next path junction marked by yellow arrows, continue ahead uphill. The path leads uphill through the woodland and reaches a wall. Cross the wall via the stile and turn left, past the ruined house. The path continues, over a footbridge and past another ruined house. You are now on the **New Precipice Walk** and after heading uphill, you soon reach another wall crossing. ▶

From this wall crossing, views can be had all the way down the Mawddach estuary to the west, south to Cadair Idris, and east towards the Arans.

Llyn Tan-y-graig, above Llanelltyd

About 500m on, a white house will come into view ahead. Follow the path as it leads to the left of the house, and past barns to the gate. At the gate turn right, up through a gap in the fence, over a stile, up a small field and over another stile, then join the grassy track going uphill on the slopes of **Foel Ispri**. The track winds uphill and is marked by several footpath signs.

The path bends right and passes to the right of a small ruin. It then follows a fence for 50m. When the fence turns left, follow it to a gate. Turn left through the gate and follow the path. At the next rise in the path, the summit of Y Garn and the Rhinogs become visible. There is a fork in the path here; continue straight ahead.

THE RHINOGYDD

Running south to north between the forest of Coed y Brenin and Tremadoc Bay, the Rhinogydd (or the anglicised 'Rhinogs') are a wild range of craggy hills centred around the two unmistakable peaks of Rhinog Fawr and Rhinog Fach. (*Rhinog* in Welsh means 'threshold', so Rhinog Fawr translates as 'great threshold'.) Although named after these two central hills, the highest point of the range is actually Y Llethr at 756m, in the grassier southern end of the ridge. Further north, the terrain becomes rougher and heather takes over from grass where it finds space to grow amongst the crags and scree that dominate the slopes.

The rocks that make up the heart of the Rhinogydd are the oldest in Snowdonia, sandstones that were laid down in the Cambrian period, 540 million years ago, along the edges of an ocean. These rocks were then uplifted 400 million years ago in the Devonian period, and experienced a further uplift 60 million years ago, after most of the mountains of the previous uplift had been eroded away.

By 50 million years ago, the landscape had taken on a structure that resembles what remains today, which subsequent ice ages and weathering has eroded, deepening valleys and moulding the mountains. Today, the Rhinogydd are a unique set of peaks that differ markedly from other mountains in Wales. A full traverse of the ridge is a long undertaking, and certainly not for walkers who like clear paths and slopes free from vegetation. You'll get a taster of this during the descent from Y Garn.

The path from here can be quite grassy and indistinct, snaking around. Continue for a few minutes and it passes through a hole in a ruined wall, then through a hole in a wall with a wooden gate. Just 10m further on, turn left; there is a stile and gate over the wall, with a footpath sign pointing towards a ruined building not far away. Cross the stile and head towards this building over marshy ground.

At the ruined building, turn right, following the wall uphill. Keep the wall on the left. You are now on the ridge leading eventually to the summit of Y Garn. Over the next 1.5km there are two intersecting walls, which you must cross by stiles. After these walls, the route reaches a stile and gate crossing the wall on the left. Cross over here so that the ridge wall is on the right.

Continue up the ridge, following the faint path for roughly 500m. There is one more wall crossing to make before the summit, over a stile which returns you to the right side of the ridge wall. Look out for this stile. If you

map continues on page 77

The south ridge of Y Garn

The whole of the Rhinogs are visible from here, as are the Moelwyns to the north, and the town of Trawsfynydd.

go too far and come to a wall corner, simply retrace your steps for 150m or so to find the stile.

Now back on the right-hand side of the ridge wall, follow it up until the wall ends, and then continue the short distance to the summit of **Y Garn**, which is marked by a small cairn. ◀

From the summit the route heads down towards the forest in the valley directly north. There is no path, and the heather and bracken can be knee-deep. Watch out for rocks and uneven ground that can be masked by the vegetation. The best route is to head approximately 300m west to avoid the crags directly north from the summit. Then turn north towards the forest.

Upon reaching the forest, turn left to follow the wall, keeping the forest on the right. Watch out for the crossing point into the forest, which is made by three long rocks through the wall, which act as steps. It can be easy to miss! Cross into the forest and follow the path, which goes straight ahead down the wide gap between the trees. The path soon reaches a post with a yellow top and then a ruined wall. Step over the wall and go through the trees the short distance to the main track, which can be seen ahead.

Turn left on the track, which leaves the forest via a cattle grid. After the grid, turn immediately right down a path, which follows the forest wall. After 50m when the path turns right to enter the forest, turn left along the faint path. This leads through undergrowth, on the left of a small brook, parallel to a ruined wall a few metres away on the right.

Shortly after a ruined building appears on the right, bear right towards it through a hole in the low ruined wall, just after a wall junction. Follow the faint path, which leads to the left side of the ruin. Continue over marshy ground and follow the path as it passes between two parallel walls close together. The path crosses the wall on the right and passes to the right of another ruined group of buildings. After passing these buildings, bear slightly left to the footbridge that crosses the **Afon Gamlan** ('meandering river').

map continues on page 78

The path continues straight uphill after the river towards **Cefn-cam**, another ruin. At the fork before the ruin, take the left side. The path heads up and soon goes through a gap in a ruined wall. It is then faint but goes gently uphill.

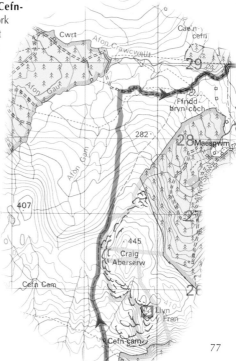

Pass through a gap in another wall shortly after and continue ahead. The path is now very indistinct and heads straight up, eventually passing through a gap in another wall. About 10 minutes after this gap, as the slope begins to level out, there is a fork in the path. Go right. The path heads towards the rocky outcrops of **Craig Aberserw** and then runs parallel to a fence. When

77

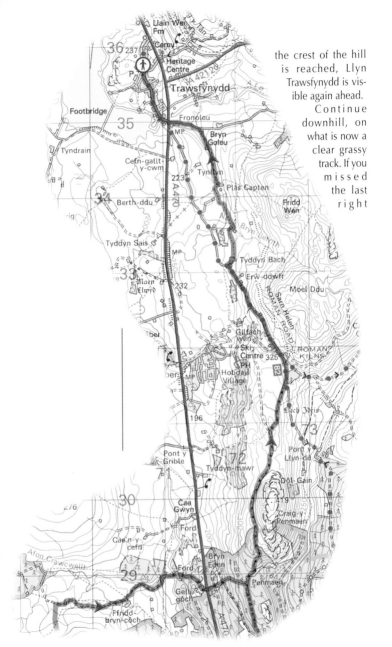

the crest of the hill is reached, Llyn Trawsfynydd is visible again ahead.

Continue downhill, on what is now a clear grassy track. If you missed the last right turn then the path eventually disappears. If you have made this error, simply head to the right over pathless ground to pick up the correct track.

The track reaches and passes through a gate in the wall ahead. Continue ahead, ignoring the yellow footpath sign that tries to send people right, off the track. The track is clear and heads downhill into the valley, swinging right as it gets further down to head towards Craig-y-Penmaen. ▶

This easy descent gives plenty of time to admire the Rhinogs – especially Rhinog Fawr.

The track leads all the way to a T-junction with a tarmac track where the farm of **Ffridd-bryn-côch** is on the right. Stay on the main track to this point and ignore tracks joining it. Turn left, away from the farm. The track goes downhill, crosses the **Afon Crawcwellt** via a bridge and bends to the right. At the fork in the track, take the left route and follow it up to the **A470**.

Cross the A470 and head straight up the footpath opposite, into the woods. Cross straight over the first track reached, and also cross the second track, which is tarmacked, continuing uphill on the footpath. At the third track, turn right and then turn left at the T-junction.

Follow Stage 2 as it heads towards the traverse next to **Craig-y-Penmaen** and on to the stage-end at **Trawsfynydd**.

Towards Trawsfynydd

STAGE 3
Trawsfynydd to Beddgelert

Start	Cross Foxes Inn, Trawsfynydd
End	Main bridge over the Colwyn, Beddgelert
Distance	18½ miles (29.5km)
Total ascent	3050ft (930m)
Time	8–9hr
Terrain	Mostly tracks, with some sections of indistinct paths and a stream crossing after Llyn Trawsfynydd. One long section of minor road before Croesor
Highest point	1023ft (312m)
Maps	OS Explorer OL18 Harlech, Porthmadog & Y Bala; OS Explorer OL17 Snowdon
Supplies	Trawsfynydd has small shops and an inn; Penrhyndeudraeth has several shops, pubs and cafés; Croesor has a café; Beddgelert has shops, pubs, cafés and an outdoor equipment shop.

Today's route passes from the south of Snowdonia to the north, across the clear dividing line of the Vale of Ffestiniog. It begins by following the edge of Llyn Trawsfynydd to the Maentwrog dam in the north, with the Rhinogs in the west and the rolling moorland of eastern Snowdonia visible across the lake. The path descends through woodland into the Vale and crosses the Afon Dwyryd as it heads west to the sea.

Beyond the town of Penrhyndeudraeth on the far side of the river, tracks lead up through forest among the foothills of the Moelwyns and over the shoulder of Cnicht – a pointed peak known as the 'Welsh Matterhorn', which reaches into the sky in the east. Meeting the Afon Glaslyn, you reach the spectacular Pass of Aberglaslyn and follow a rocky path next to the river into Beddgelert, a fantastic end to the day.

From the main road in **Trawsfynydd**, follow the road Cefn Gwyn, which is opposite the Cross Foxes inn. Turn right past the playground and then right down a track with a

The bridge over Llyn Trawsfynydd

footpath sign. Another track leads up a small hill, which leads to a dead end at the war memorial. ▸

Once on the track, continue until a footpath sign sends you left across a field and down to the long **footbridge** over Llyn Trawsfynydd. Once over the bridge, drop down to the road and turn right. At the next road fork, turn right again to keep on the road that traverses round the western side of the lake.

If you have time, head up to the memorial for a view of the lake ahead.

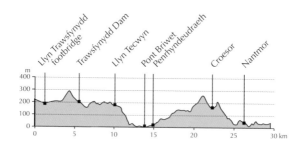

81

At **Moelfryn** ('bare-topped hill'), the road ends and three tarmacked tracks lie ahead. Take the central track, marked with a footpath and cycle path sign, which bears left off the road. (The other two tracks are private drives and should be obvious.)

The track becomes a gravelled path uphill, only recently built and easy to follow. As it heads downhill, the track passes to the left of **Coed y Rhygen**. Below this woodland on the right lies the northern edge of the lake. Follow the path all the way to the Maentwrog dam. At the gate that leads onto the dam, turn left onto a footpath that is marked with a sign. ◄

If you want to go onto the dam to admire the view down the gorge of the Afon Prysor, remember to come back to this point.

The path heads down to the edge of the gorge and turns left, crossing an open area towards the woodland of Coed Llennyrch. When the path reaches a wall, you can either crawl through the hole provided, or

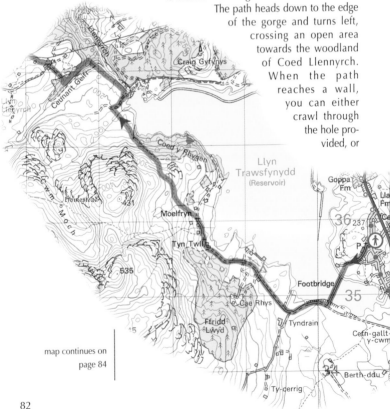

map continues on page 84

head up the wall approximately 50m and pass through the larger gap. Rejoin the path and continue ahead, keeping the gorge on the right.

Descend through the woods to a stream and cross it. There is no bridge but there are plenty of stones to walk on. The path continues straight up the opposite bank. At the top of the bank, turn left at the path junction.

This path soon reaches a gap through a ruined wall where the path seems to end. Go through the gap and bear right, diagonally uphill. The path soon re-emerges and then joins another path, which traverses the slope near the top. Continue following this path, which has great views down to the gorge on the left.

The path bears right, away from the stream and comes to a T-junction with another path, where there are yellow footpath signs on a tree. Turn right and go through the gate into the field beyond.

Follow the grassy path, which bears left and follows a fence. It soon reaches a cluster of buildings, with a pylon ahead. ▸ Continue in the same direction

Through the woods of Coed Llennyrch

There is a great view back towards the Maentwrog dam from these buildings.

past all the buildings and turn left onto a grassy track, which leads through a fence and then a ruined wall. The track continues round the small hillside and reaches another fence.

Beyond the fence gap, go straight ahead on the grassy path across the field, keeping the ruined building on the left. Head through the hole in the wall on the right-hand side of the pylon and enter the woodland. The path is now distinct and leads straight on.

After a hole in the next fence, bear right towards a stile, which crosses a wall into the conifer forest of **Coed Felinrhyd**. Continue ahead along this path. At the path fork in the forest, go right. At the major track, turn left, and at the next junction, where the main track swings right, turn left onto the grassy track.

Continue along this track until you reach a wall on the right. Follow the footpath along it, and soon a footpath sign sends you downhill, still following the wall. The route goes through a gate and heads out over an open area, with crags on the right. The path then ascends through a wall and follows a fence through another gate into the woods. At the track in the woods, turn right. As this track bends left you can see the crags of Moel Tecwyn ahead.

map continues on page 87

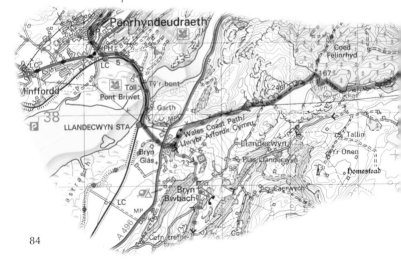

At the junction, turn left, and then left again after 50m, down the footpath. The path passes to the right of **Llyn Tecwyn** and once past it you can see the sea ahead in the distance.

Once past the lake, turn right onto the path that leads downhill. Ignore the track ahead, which goes uphill. You are now descending into the Vale of Ffestiniog and the estuary of the Afon Glaslyn ('river of the green lake').

> Separating south and north Snowdonia, the **Vale of Ffestiniog** ('valley of the land of Ffestin') runs from the town of Blaenau Ffestiniog ('heads of valleys in the land of Ffestin') in the eastern hills down to the sea at Tremadoc Bay. At its heart is the Afon Dwyryd and the Ffestiniog railway, which used to carry slate from the mines around Blaenau Ffestiniog to the port at Porthmadog ('Madoc's harbour'), to be shipped to the rest of Britain and the world. Today this narrow gauge line has been reopened to carry travellers and is an excellent way of seeing the valley, with its woodland-crowded slopes slowly giving way to the sands of the estuary.

The path reaches the road in **Bryn Glâs** ('green hill') after passing through a gate and to the left of a house. Turn right to go downhill, cross the **A496** and go straight down the road ahead towards the river.

Follow the pavement on this road over the river via **Pont Briwet**; the road shares the bridge with the railway line. Continue to Penrhyndeudraeth railway station. At the station, turn right up the road to the centre of **Penrhyndeudraeth**. At the crossroads, go straight ahead along the road signposted to Beddgelert. Turn right immediately after the car park/recycling centre. Follow the road past terraced houses on the left, and then a field on the right.

After the field, the road swings right, then left again. Take the first street on the left; there is a sign ahead marking the street of Pant Heulog.

Turn right down Pant Heulog, and at the end of this short street take the footpath between hedges, which continues on, slightly on the right-hand side. After 50m, turn left onto a connecting footpath, which goes up to the road.

Turn right on the road and soon pass alongside the narrow gauge railway lines of the **Ffestiniog railway**. Cross the tracks when they cross the road and almost immediately take the first right down a minor road marked as a dead end. Follow this road for some time.

There is a track fork at the entrance to Rhiw Goch ('red hillside'); continue straight ahead along the tarmacked track. At the cluster of houses, keep left along the track through three gates. After the third gate continue ahead along the grassy track leading towards woodland. After 50m there is a path junction, but keep straight on along the track going gently uphill.

Leaving Coed Llyn y Garnedd

The track enters the forest of **Coed Llyn y Garnedd** via a stile. About 50m after entering the wood, bear left

at the fork, following the footpath signs. This well-defined path continues for 1km and is distinct.

The path leaves the forest onto open hillside, where it is grassy but well defined. Keep the forest on the right and follow the footpath arrows. The path bends slightly left after a marsh and reaches a gate, from where you can see the slopes of Moelwyn Bach ('little bare hill') ahead. Soon after this gate the path reaches the B4410 at the entrance to **Rhyd** ('ford' or 'stream').

Turn right to go downhill into Rhyd and take the first track on the left, in the middle of the village, just past the house with white metal railings, before the road turns right. The track bends right then left. After passing the dark blue barn on the right, go straight ahead through two gates when the track bends left. Follow the path, which soon bends left through another gate and then across an open field.

The path reaches a track. Turn right on the track and follow the path straight on past the house and uphill through the field ahead. There are footpath signs in some places. The path goes uphill into woodland and soon reaches the minor road at **Ogof Llechwyn**.

Turn left and walk along the road all the way to **Croesor**

map continues on page 89

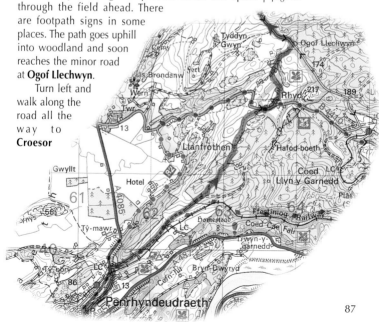

One of the best views of the mountain of Cnicht ('knight') can be had from the final descent into Croesor.

('many crosses'). There are a few gates on this road. ◄ Once in Croesor, go ahead at the crossroads, pass the car park and continue straight along the road as it goes uphill out of the village. When the road ends, go through the gate straight ahead and continue along the track into the woods.

When the track leaves the woodland, continue straight ahead at the fork, ignoring the right-hand turn leading to Cnicht. On the left you can see Moel Hebog ('bald hill of the hawk'), which stands above Beddgelert. Follow the track

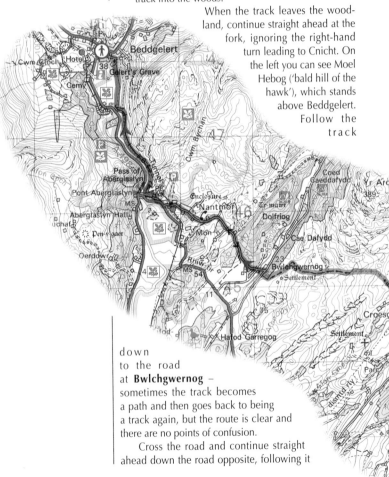

down
to the road
at **Bwlchgwernog** –
sometimes the track becomes
a path and then goes back to being
a track again, but the route is clear and
there are no points of confusion.

Cross the road and continue straight
ahead down the road opposite, following it

to **Nantmor**. Once over the railway line, this road reaches the main road of the A4085. Turn right along the road past one house and turn right into the National Trust **car park** at Aberglaslyn.

Go through the car park and turn left through the gate on the left of the toilet block. Follow the path ahead, signed to Aberglaslyn. When this path reaches the Afon Glaslyn at **Pont Aberglaslyn**, turn right to follow the path alongside the river, heading upstream through the **Pass of Aberglaslyn**. This rocky trail can be slippery and care must be taken.

Cross the river at the footbridge next to the railway bridge and continue following the riverside path on

Following the Afon Glaslyn to Beddgelert

89

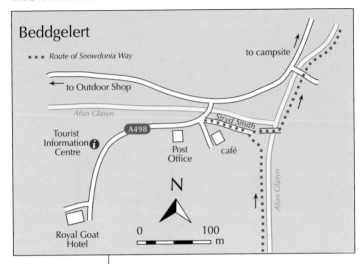

The hill ahead is Yr Aran, one of the peaks of Snowdon, so you are right in the heart of Snowdonia.

the other side. Beddgelert is now in view ahead. Turn left at the next gate to visit **Gelert's Grave** and statue, and continue on the footpath towards the town. Turn left at the road to reach the main bridge over the Colwyn and the centre of **Beddgelert**. ◀

BEDDGELERT

There is no place in Snowdonia that feels more like an Alpine village than Beddgelert, surrounded on all sides by steep slopes and located at the sometimes turbulent meeting point of the Afon Colwyn and Afon Glaslyn, before they plunge south to the Pass of Aberglaslyn.

The village used to be one of the main starting points for walkers wishing to climb Snowdon, which lies just to the north, and in the many travelogues of the 17th to 19th centuries it is nearly always the place the writers would come to find guides. Wordsworth was one of these, and visited in 1805 – an event that is recorded in his poem *The Prelude*. If you are on the high route of the Snowdonia Way, you should know that doing a Snowdon ascent from Beddgelert is a tradition that goes back to the very first travellers.

The village is famous for the legend of Gelert, a hound owned by Llewelyn the Great. The story goes that one day Llewelyn went out hunting, leaving Gelert in charge of his baby son. On his return, he found the room in disarray, no sign of his son, and Gelert covered in blood. Immediately thinking the dog had killed his child, he thrust his sword through Gelert. At the sound of the dog's dying howl, Llewelyn heard a baby crying from beneath the upturned cot. He turned it over to find his son, safe, next to the body of a dead wolf. Realising that Gelert had killed the wolf to protect his son, Llewelyn was filled with remorse and built a memorial to Gelert outside the village.

Unfortunately, poetic as the story is, it was made up in the 18th century by David Pritchard, the manager of the Royal Goat Hotel, to bring more tourists to the village. The 'grave' still stands outside the village, with a statue of Gelert nearby. The name Beddgelert in fact means 'the grave of Saint Celert', who was hopefully modest enough not to mind being usurped by a fictional hound.

STAGE 3A

Trawsfynydd to Penrhyndeudraeth
(mountain route)

Start	Cross Foxes Inn, Trawsfynydd
End	Main crossroads, Penrhyndeudraeth
Distance	11¾ miles (18.9km)
Total ascent	2855ft (870m)
Time	6–7hr
Terrain	A short section of road followed by marshy ground with an indistinct path. The hill-paths are faint and not always easy to follow. Once back into the valley there are tracks and minor road
Summits	Moel Ysgyfarnogod (2044ft/623m)
Maps	OS Explorer OL18 Harlech, Porthmadog & Y Bala
Supplies	Trawsfynydd has a few small shops and an inn; Penrhyndeudraeth has a selection of shops, pubs and cafés.

Starting by crossing the long bridge over Llyn Trawsfynydd, today's route heads through the marsh east of the Rhinogs. Slowly ascending, the path reaches the crest of the ridge south of Craig Ddrwg before heading north over the intricate craggy summit area of Moel Ysgyfarnogod. There are a lot of minor summits to explore and plenty of rock features to scramble over or work your way round. Whatever the weather here, it's a great little world all of its own, and the most fun can be had by exploring the rock features and discovering a previously unseen perspective.

From the summit of Moel Ysgyfarnogod, the route heads down a grassy gully, on pathless terrain that leads gently towards the Vale of Ffestiniog and across the Afon Dwyryd, the dividing line between north and south Snowdonia.

From the main road in **Trawsfynydd**, follow the road Cefn Gwyn, which is opposite the Cross Foxes Inn. Turn right past the playground and then right down a track with a footpath sign. Another track leads up a small hill, which leads to a dead end at the war memorial.

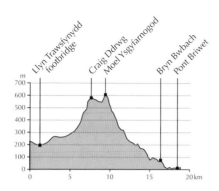

Once on the track, continue until a footpath sign sends you left across a field and down to the long **footbridge** over Llyn Trawsfynydd. Cross the bridge and turn right onto the road on the other side. At the road fork, turn left and follow the road. There's a sharp right bend at the entrance to **Ty-cerrig**; don't accidentally head down their driveway.

The road climbs then flattens out. Continue on it past the track

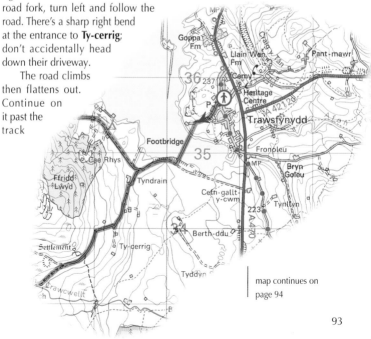

map continues on page 94

93

next to the metal sheep pens. The road descends slightly. Take the next left onto the grassy track towards the barns at Wern-fâch; there's a footpath sign on a metal post. ◄

This track can be marshy, as can the whole of the section following the stream. Just try to enjoy it!

As the track approaches the barn, go left to cross the footbridge of the **Afon Crawcwellt**. Continue ahead for 20m to the post with the yellow arrows. Turn right and follow the faint path towards the house further up the valley. There's a sign to Cwm Bychan.

Cross two stiles, staying on the left side of the stream. The path passes to the right side of the house, then continues following the stream through a gate. The going gets less marshy after the house, but as there are several faint paths it's best to look around for the driest route.

The path heads towards the left-hand side of Craig Ddrwg, the crag ahead, where there is a pass between these crags and Craig Wion, which is on the left. The path bears left towards the pass along with the stream and a wall, which follows the stream. The wall becomes a fence, and then a wall again further up.

map continues on page 97

Once through the marshiest bits the ground becomes heathery; go through a gate in an intersecting wall and continue following

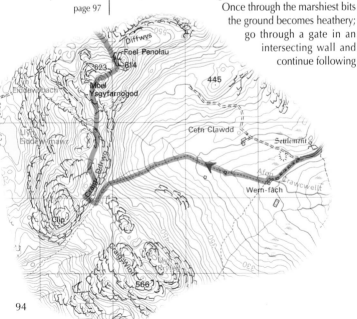

94

the path uphill. Stay near to the wall on the right for the best path.

When the wall turns right, keep straight on towards the pass. Just before the crest of the pass, turn right at a fork in the path and ascend this path to cross a stile on the slope on the right. The path is steep and rocky and heads up between crags to the top of **Craig Ddrwg**. (If you miss the first fork you will also get to a stile, but will then start going downhill over the other side of the pass. If you find yourself going downhill, you've gone the wrong way.)

The path begins to level out on Craig Ddrwg and bears right to follow the ridge line. This path snakes around all the way to the summit of Moel Ysgyfarnogod ('bare hill of hares') to take the easiest route through the crags, although it is not always clear. Follow it as best you can or pick your own way. There is probably room for some fun scrambling if you have the time.

The summit of **Moel Ysgyfarnogod** has a trig point, which is useful if it's misty as there are many false summits around. The easiest ascent is by skirting round to the north-west. From the summit, descend north-east

Heading along the ridge to Moel Ysgyfarnogod

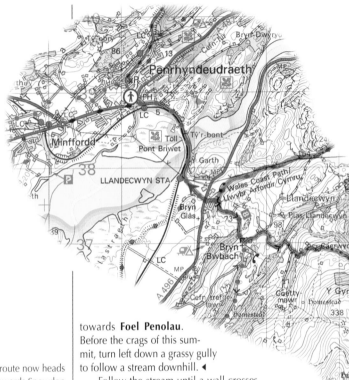

The route now heads towards Snowdon and the Nantlle Ridge, which stand out in the distance.

towards **Foel Penolau**.
Before the crags of this summit, turn left down a grassy gully to follow a stream downhill. ◄

Follow the stream until a wall crosses it, blocking the way down. About 40m before this wall, a faint path crosses the slope; turn right onto this path, which runs parallel to the wall. The path crosses a stile across an intersecting wall, and shortly after, passes through a gap in the next intersecting wall. Go ahead, where the path goes downhill diagonally, soon reaching another path at a T-junction next to the edge of a small woodland. Turn left, downhill through the woodland.

Once through the woodland, the path follows the wall, traversing the slope. Do not be tempted through a hole in the wall on the right, which leads to the farm Nant-Pasgan. After crossing a stream, head onwards to

The Afon Dwyryd estuary

a ruined house, keeping the ruined wall on the right.

At the ruin, turn right to cross the stone slab bridge and follow the path ahead to a track. Turn left and follow the track. Pass through the riding centre at **Caerwych** and continue winding downhill. At the next junction, continue ahead downhill.

At the next road junction, turn left. The road goes around a small lake and arrives at a junction with a red phone-box and postbox at **Bryn Bwbach**. Turn right and follow the road down to the main road. Cross straight over and continue on the road towards **Pont Briwet** and the river. ▶

Cross the bridge, and continue on the other side until **Penrhyndeudraeth station** appears on the left. Turn right

The river beneath is the Afon Dwyryd, which joins the Afon Glaslyn further west before reaching the sea.

97

up the road opposite to arrive at the main crossroads in the centre of town.

PENRHYNDEUDRAETH

The tranquil setting of the village of Penrhyndeudraeth ('headland of two beaches') is testament to the ability of nature to reclaim a post-industrial landscape: this used to be the site of the largest explosives works in Europe. It began in 1865, when a factory making guncotton (nitrocellulose) was established at Gwaith Powdwr just outside the village. After a massive explosion on the site in 1915, the site was taken over by another explosives company under Imperial Chemical Industries, who manufactured explosives for use in both world wars.

The demand for explosives for coal mining increased the fortunes of the site, which was able to manufacture a safer type of explosives, for use in the gas-filled mines. This peaked in 1970, but the downturn in mining and the availability of cheap imports led to the decline and eventual closure of the works in 1995. In 1998 the site was given to the North Wales Wildlife Trust and is now a nature reserve. You will pass it on the right-hand side after crossing the estuary. There are several paths leading you through the site and many of the old works buildings are still there to explore. The reserve is known for the lesser horseshoe bat and the nightjar, as well as other species.

Before the establishment of the first works in 1865, the village had only been in its current form for less than a decade; previously there was a much smaller settlement called Upper Penrhyn. Most of the land for the new town was created by draining marsh, and there used to be a lake where the High Street is today; echoes of this can still be seen in the street and terrace names, such as Glanllyn ('lakeside').

STAGE 3B

Penrhyndeudraeth to Beddgelert
(mountain route)

Start	Main crossroads, Penrhyndeudraeth
End	Bridge over the Colwyn, Beddgelert
Distance	15¾ miles (25.2km)
Total ascent	4495ft (1370m)
Time	7–8hr
Terrain	Forest paths before a section of minor road, then mountain paths which are sometimes faint. Once down Cnicht, distinct track and minor road, with a riverside path to finish
Summits	Moelwyn Mawr (2526ft/770m), Cnicht (2260ft/689m)
Maps	OS Explorer OL18 Harlech, Porthmadog & Y Bala; OS Explorer OL17 Snowdon
Supplies	Both Penrhyndeudraeth and Beddgelert have a selection of shops, pubs and cafés. Beddgelert has an outdoor equipment shop.

The Moelwyns are a vast plateau of peaks, lakes and rocky spurs that rise up between the Vale of Ffestiniog and the higher peaks to the north. This route leads through the forest on the edges of Penrhyndeudraeth and up onto the plateau via the highest peak in the area, Moelwyn Mawr. Paths then lead down through the spoil tips and ruins of abandoned slate mines towards the famous peak of Cnicht, known as the Welsh Matterhorn for it's pointed outline.

The descent from the summit of Cnicht is steep at first but then leads gently down a grassy ridge, with the sea in full view ahead and the long arm of the Llyn peninsula reaching away into the distance. Joining tracks and veering north, the route now heads towards the dramatic Pass of Aberglaslyn, where it follows the river up into Beddgelert, a mountain village at the heart of Snowdonia.

Follow Stage 3 from the main crossroads in **Penrhyndeudraeth** to **Ogof Llechwyn**, then turn left onto

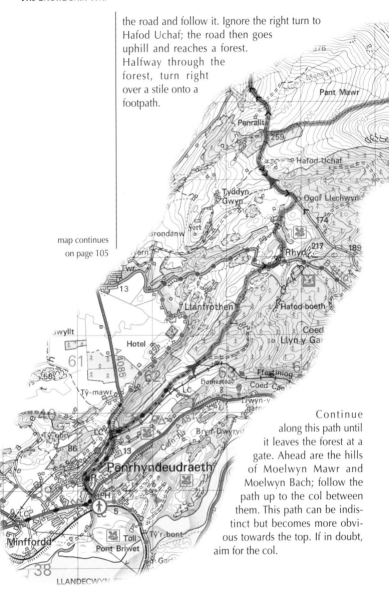

the road and follow it. Ignore the right turn to Hafod Uchaf; the road then goes uphill and reaches a forest. Halfway through the forest, turn right over a stile onto a footpath.

map continues on page 105

Continue along this path until it leaves the forest at a gate. Ahead are the hills of Moelwyn Mawr and Moelwyn Bach; follow the path up to the col between them. This path can be indistinct but becomes more obvious towards the top. If in doubt, aim for the col.

From the col, the reservoir of Llyn Stwlan can be seen below, and further away the slate mining town of Blaenau Ffestiniog. Turn left on the col up the steep slope of Moelwyn Mawr. The path is rocky, and there is an impressively large quartz vein towards the top of the first section.

The rocky false summit reached is actually **Craigysgafn** ('mild crag'), with the rounded summit of Moelwyn Mawr now visible ahead. Follow the path on up to the summit of **Moelwyn Mawr**, where there is a trig point.

THE MOELWYNION

The range of hills between the Vale of Ffestiniog and Nantgwynant are the Moelwynion (anglicised to 'The Moelwyns'). In the north, they drop down to the Bwlch y Rhediad before rising to Moel Siabod. Aside from Moel Siabod ('shapely hill'), the two highest peaks are Moelwyn Mawr ('great white hill') and Moelwyn Bach ('little white hill'), which the range is named after. One of the more famous peaks is Cnicht, which gets its name, meaning 'knight', from the appearance of its pyramidal summit from Porthmadog and the coast. Nowadays, its precipitous western side has earned it the nickname 'The Welsh Matterhorn', after the famous Swiss mountain.

Slate quarrying took place on the Moelwynion on a big scale, especially in the land just to the north of Moelwyn Mawr, where the Croesor and Rhosydd works had frequent extraction above 500m. These caverns, at the head of the Croesor valley, were later used to store explosives after the slate mining ceased. Down towards Blaenau Ffestiniog, the Cwmorthin quarry takes up the whole of the lower hillside. These days, despite the industrial past, the solitude of the many small lakes spread over the Moelwynion make them a popular site for wild camping.

From the summit, double back on yourself to find the start of the north-east ridge. Heading back from the summit trig point towards Blaenau Ffestiniog, bear left and

The quartz vein near the top of Moelwyn Mawr

pick up the ridge, which descends towards the Moelwyn plateau. The path goes to the right of a distinctive knoll at the end of the ridge; there are mine workings ahead and on the right.

Soon the path follows a fence. When the fence turns left, cross the stile ahead and continue on the

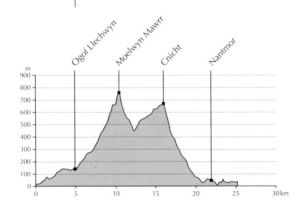

path straight on towards the spoil tip. Follow the path as it bends left when it reaches the edge of the spoil and passes the ruins of old mine buildings. About 100m further on you pass another ruin, where the path bends right and heads between what look like the stumps of two thick walls.

Ruined building from the old slate mines

The path then descends on a steep stony path along one of the old inclines. It leads down past a pool to the flat area covered with the former buildings of the quarry. Go straight across this flat area through the buildings and mine detritus towards a stream on the other side.

Just before the stream, a pile of stones marks the start of a path, which bears up to the left. Follow the path up; it is indistinct, but soon bears right and follows a fence. Continue following the fence to **Llyn Cwm-corsiog**. Turn left through the gate next to the lake and continue along the path.

The path snakes across the slopes, with Cnicht visible ahead on the left. The route is sometimes faint, but keep contouring across marshy bits and around crags. The path eventually rises up to the crest of the hill just before **Llyn yr Adar**. There's a cairn to mark this high point and the

This section gives an excellent impression of what the Moelwyn plateau is like, undulating and frequently confusing even to experienced navigators.

lake is visible ahead. If in doubt, make your own way there doing the best you can. ◄

At the crest with Llyn yr Adar ahead, turn south-west (left) and head towards Cnicht. The slope starts wide and grassy, but eventually narrows to the stony summit ridge. Cnicht has two tops, the furthest one from this direction being the summit.

From the summit of **Cnicht**, descend off the far end, continuing south-west. The initial section is quite rocky and feels like a scramble. Stick to the crest of the ridge. The best route is to follow the path that soon drops off the left side and then continues down with the crest of the ridge on the right. (The paths that continue on the right of the ridge crest lead to a steep scramble down, which can be dangerous when wet.)

This scrambly section ends on a grassy platform with a cairn. Continue descending the ridge path, and roughly 800m further down, the

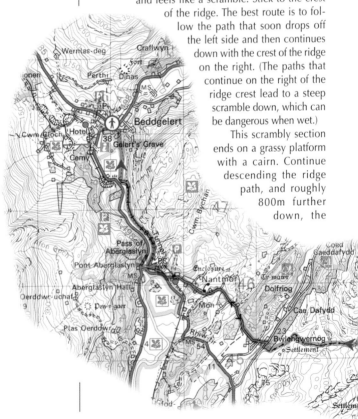

Looking back at Cnicht

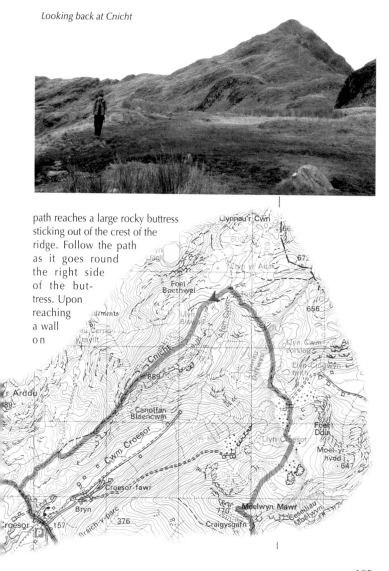

path reaches a large rocky buttress
sticking out of the crest of the
ridge. Follow the path
as it goes round
the right side
of the but-
tress. Upon
reaching
a wall
on

Beddgelert and the Afon Glaslyn

the far side, cross the stile to continue ahead down the ridge on a grassy path.

Continue down the ridge for a few hundred metres to reach another wall, where the path swings right through a gate and leaves the ridge. At the Y-junction immediately afterwards, take either option as they meet up soon after. The path descends and soon becomes a stony track.

As this track nears the woodland ahead, it reaches a junction with another track. Turn right onto this track and follow it to **Bwlchgwernog**, and from there follow Stage 3 to **Beddgelert**.

STAGE 4

Beddgelert to Dolwyddelan

Start	Bridge over the Colwyn, Beddgelert
End	Gwydyr Hotel, Dolwyddelan
Distance	12¾ miles (20.6km)
Total ascent	2625ft (800m)
Time	6–7hr
Terrain	Distinct river, lakeside and mountain paths. Once over the Bwlch y Rhediad, some boggy path and several long sections of stony track
Highest point	1253ft (382m)
Maps	OS Explorer OL18 Harlech, Porthmadog & Y Bala; OS Explorer OL17 Snowdon
Supplies	Beddgelert has a selection of shops and cafés; Dolwyddelan has a shop and pubs.

Leaving Beddgelert, the first half of the route winds its way up the valley of Nantgwynant. It passes through small woodlands and follows the river, past the serene mountain lakes of Llyn Dinas and Llyn Gwynant, the slopes of Snowdon towering up in the north. Then begins the ascent up to the pass of Bwlch y Rhediad, which is steep but short and reveals a view back down Nantgwynant and to the summit of Snowdon itself.

Now in much wilder terrain, the route heads into open moorland on its way down to the valley of the Afon Lledr. This area has much more forest cover than most of north Snowdonia, and the first of several large plantations appears on the left, on the slopes of Moel Siabod. Entering the valley, the route passes next to Dolwyddelan Castle – one of the castles built by Llewelyn the Great – before dropping down to Dolwyddelan itself.

From the main road bridge in the centre of **Beddgelert**, face downstream and take the dead-end road on the right-hand side of the river, leading past the craft centre and over the footbridge. Head left, still following the river. Cross the small road and go through the gate onto a path;

The route stays on the right-hand side of the river all the way to Llyn Dinas.

map continues on page 112

cross another gate and continue on the path, which is now laid with flagstones. ◄

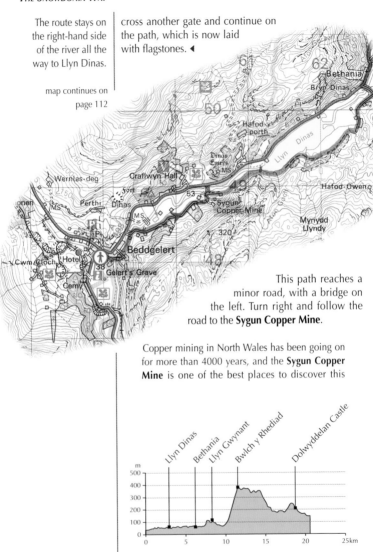

This path reaches a minor road, with a bridge on the left. Turn right and follow the road to the **Sygun Copper Mine**.

Copper mining in North Wales has been going on for more than 4000 years, and the **Sygun Copper Mine** is one of the best places to discover this history. Closed in 1903, the mine is now fully open to the public via a walking tour underground, and outdoor exhibits. The underground tour takes approximately 40 minutes. Open from 10 February to 10 November, 9.30am–5pm in summertime and 10am–4pm in wintertime. Also open during the New Years Day week (www.syguncopper mine.co.uk).

At the mine, the road swings left. Follow it round towards the bridge, following the sign for the Lakeside Walk. Before the bridge, turn right along the track, which keeps you on the right-hand side of the river, where there is a footpath sign.

DINAS EMRYS

The summit of this rocky wooded hill on the outskirts of Beddgelert has been occupied as a fort during several periods from the Iron Age to the Middle Ages, and it occupies an obvious defensive site in the heart of Snowdonia. Its most famous visitor, however, is Merlin – later to be associated with King Arthur – and the story of Dinas Emrys is his first appearance.

The tale goes that Vortigern, a fifth-century British king who had fled to Wales during his fight against the Saxons, was attempting to build a fort on Dinas Emrys. But every time his builders laid the first stones of the fort, they would come back the next day and find what they had built destroyed. Vortigern asked his court wizards to solve the mystery, and they concluded that the place was cursed, and only by sprinkling the blood of a fatherless boy upon the hill would Vortigern be able to build his fort. Searching the country, they found Merddyn Emrys, or Merlin, who was brought before Vortigern.

In order to avoid being sacrificed, Merlin convinced Vortigern that he could solve the problem by excavating the summit. Vortigern agreed and the work proceeded until a pool was uncovered; Merlin then drained the pool and within it was found an urn containing two sleeping dragons, one red and one white. The dragons awoke and began fighting; eventually the red dragon gained the upper hand and chased the white dragon away. Merlin interpreted this as foreseeing a time when the Britons would rise up and finally drive the Saxons from their land. Vortigern's fort was eventually completed and Merlin began his long career as our most famous wizard.

This story is also one of the legends behind the red dragon's place on the Welsh flag, and recent archaeological work on Dinas Emrys has found evidence of structures dating from the fifth century, which place it around the time of Vortigern. Today you can walk to the summit of the hill, where the major visible structure is the base of a rectangular building, perhaps constructed by Llewelyn the Great in the Middle Ages.

Llyn Dinas, the last of four lakes on the Afon Glaslyn, which starts high on Snowdon and tumbles down to the sea near Porthmadog

As you leave the small stand of trees, the small hill of Dinas Emrys will appear on your left.

The path arrives at **Llyn Dinas** ('lake of the hillfort') and crosses a gate to begin going round the right side of the lake. At a split in the path almost immediately after the gate, take the left fork. Cross the footbridge over the **Afon Goch** ('red river'), admiring the impressive cascade on your right.

Cross through a wall to enter the National Trust woodland of Llyndy Isaf and follow the path ahead next to the lakeshore. The path winds its way past the lake, through open fields and woodland, and eventually reaches farm buildings. Continue ahead along the main track past the buildings, all the way to a T-junction with a minor road.

Turn left on this road to cross the river and reach the A498. Turn right, crossing the road to the safer side through the car park to **Bethania**. After passing the group of buildings, including a café, turn left onto the minor road signposted Hafod y llan and follow it for a few hundred metres. Turn right over the footbridge and follow the path, which runs next to the Afon Glaslyn. This path is not marked on OS maps.

The path leads over another footbridge, turns left and then right to enter a field. Head diagonally up to the far corner of the field, keeping the river on the right. Before the far corner, on reaching a track, turn right and follow the track through a gap in the wall. Continue along it across two more fields, soon reaching a stone building.

The track then turns left away from the river and begins to swing right towards a house. On this bend, you will see a clump of trees on a rocky mound. Just before these trees, a path goes left off the track, in-between the trees and a small stream. Although not obvious at first, it soon becomes clear. Head uphill, bearing right towards and through a hole in the wall ahead. Keep the outcrop of **Penmaen-brith** on the right and follow the path up to the minor pass. From this high point, Llyn Gwynant ('lake in a fair valley') comes into view, and the path heads down towards it.

The path leads to a woodland, across two small streams and up to a rocky knoll with fantastic views over the lake. The path now stays high above the lake, heading north-east; ignore a path on your right which heads down to the shore.

The path descends to the Nantgwynant **campsite** at the end of the lake, then follows a mossy stone wall past huge boulders and a small cave. When a stone footbridge

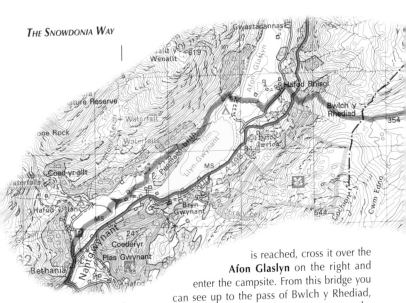

is reached, cross it over the **Afon Glaslyn** on the right and enter the campsite. From this bridge you can see up to the pass of Bwlch y Rhediad, where you are heading, marked by a lone crag on the low point of the ridge.

Go straight ahead across the first field, towards a gate with a footpath sign leading onwards. Pass through this gate, cross a stream and then go through another g ate into a big field. Head straight across this field, keeping the fence on your right. Cross the stile, then a stream, than another stile into another field. Keep straight ahead, with the fence on the right, to a final stile and the road. There are footpath signs frequently across these fields.

On the road, turn left and follow the road to the houses at **Hafod Rhisgl**. Pass the track leading to houses on the left, and go through the first gate on the right, up a rocky path. The footpath becomes grassy and steep and leads up to the A498, where there are great views back over Llyn Gwynant. From the road, the path continues uphill on the other side, slightly to the left. The path enters a woodland and continues uphill; when the path forks, take the right fork, which leads up. There are a few small footpath signs.

The route leaves the woodland and reaches the open hillside. When it reaches a wall, ignore the metal gate and head towards the wooden stile further on. Go over this stile and follow the path bearing right uphill, leading you to the **Bwlch y Rhediad**. Head straight on over the top and cross the stile, to continue ahead.

The path descends a short way before bearing left to traverse the hillside beneath Carnedd y Cribau. There are regular footpath signs along this path. ▶ A small stand of trees will appear ahead on the right-hand side, and there are the remains of a small ruin. Continue past the ruin, and also past a small wooden post with yellow arrows, to a second

map continues on page 114

This valley is distinctly different from the previous one, and the contrast between the tranquil route next to Llyn Dinas and the wild bowl of Cwm Edno on the right is striking.

Snowdon from the Bwlch y Rhediad

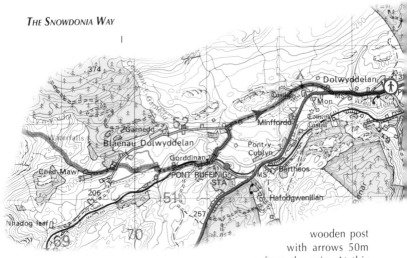

wooden post
with arrows 50m
on from the ruin. At this
point turn right and head straight
downhill, following the grassy path to the stream of the
Ceunant Ty'n-y-ddol.

Cross the footbridge and head up the path opposite,
over a stile. After another 50m the path swings left and
becomes distinct, traversing the hillside. It becomes a
track, which can be followed down to the farm at **Coed
Mawr** ('big woodland').

Turn left onto the track through the farm and follow the
tarmac track ahead to the road. At the road, go through the
gate ahead and cross the field to the gate with the yellow
arrow. Continue on the faint path over the small mound to
the fence corner ahead, also with a yellow arrow.

Follow the fence, on the right of the pool. When
the fence turns left, keep straight ahead towards the
footbridge. Cross the bridge and turn left after the stile
towards another bridge. Follow the track after this bridge
to cross the railway bridge, then follow the track left
through the farm at **Gorddinan** to the road.

Turn left on the road and follow it up to the farm
ahead on the slope. When amongst the farm buildings,
as the road turns left, turn right down a track past barns,
where there is a metal footpath sign.

Go through the gate, over a stile, and follow a footpath sign through another gate. This track leads through fields and then descends towards **Dolwyddelan Castle**, passing to the left of it. Keep following this track downhill. When it hairpins right, keep straight ahead, through the gate. Descend this track to the road, the A470. Turn left on the road, where there is a footpath, and arrive in **Dolwyddelan**. The Gwydyr Hotel is on the road in the middle of the village, and to the right is the Spar. ▸

If your accommodation is in the next village of Pont-y-pant, there is a footpath on the side of the road all the way there.

DOLWYDDELAN

Named after Saint Gwyddelan, a fifth-century Irish missionary, the village of Dolwyddelan ('meadow of Gwyddelan') sits alongside the A470 and the Afon Lledr. The church of Saint Gwyddelan was built in around 1500, replacing an earlier structure, and the old bell was said to have been brought over from Ireland by Gwyddelan himself. Later, it became a slate mining village, and the old spoil tips can be seen on the far side of the valley, slowly being enveloped by woodland. You can find out more about the village at www.dolwyddelan.org.

The impressive Dolwyddelan Castle, standing above the Lledr valley, is said to have been the birthplace of Llewelyn the Great, although the original structure has been dated back to the early 13th century and Llewelyn was born in the 1170s. Evidence for an earlier structure has been found in the form of an earth mound on the other side of the road, and if this building was in fact Llewelyn's birthplace, then Dolwyddelan was almost certainly built by him.

During Llewelyn ap Gruffudd's revolt against Edward I, the castle was lost in 1283, perhaps by treachery, but was of little use to Edward as it was far from the sea. It fell into disuse and was abandoned in 1290, although Edward did build a second tower and used it as a base for a winter campaign where his troops were fitted with white tunics as camouflage. Later modifications date from its revival in the 15th century and then substantial reconstruction in the middle of the 19th century, including the addition of the battlements.

The site is open to explore from April to September 10am–5pm Mon–Sat and 11.30am–4pm Sun; also October to March 10am–4pm Mon–Sat and 11.30am–4pm Sun. Call Cadw on 01690 750366.

Dolwyddelan Castle

STAGE 4A

Beddgelert to Pen-y-Pass
(mountain route)

Start	Bridge over the Colwyn, Beddgelert
End	Pen-y-Pass
Distance	11¼ miles (17.9km)
Total ascent	4855ft (1480m)
Time	6–7hr
Terrain	Mountain paths, which are distinct, but as there are many of them on Snowdon the skill is in making sure you're on the right one
Summits	Snowdon (3560ft/1085m)
Maps	OS Explorer OL17 Snowdon
Supplies	Beddgelert has a selection of shops, cafés and pubs. There is a café on the summit of Snowdon. Pen-y-Pass has a café and a Youth Hostel, which also contains a restaurant. Further down the path past Pen-y-Pass is the Hotel of Pen-y-Gwryd.

This is it, the journey to the summit of Snowdon! From Beddgelert, the trail winds its way up the valley of Nantgwynant past Llyn Dinas and through woodland, before turning up into Cwm Llan. Leaving the valleys behind, the route climbs into this mighty glacial bowl and then leads up to Bwlch Cwm Llan, the low point at the end of the south ridge of Snowdon.

The journey up the south ridge is dramatic, the ridge sometimes narrow, with views down to mountains on both sides. From the summit, the route follows the Pyg Track down to Pen-y-Pass – a popular rocky route through another of the great valleys of Snowdon, Cwm Glaslyn. Pen-y-Pass itself is a cluster of buildings that sits at the head of the Llanberis Pass, a true mountain hostel.

From **Beddgelert**, follow Stage 4 directions to **Bethania** and turn left down the minor road signposted Hafod y llan. Go up the stone steps to enter the woodland and

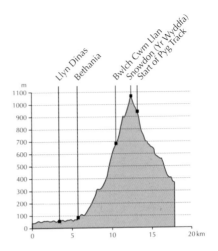

follow the path through it. At the track junction after the wood, turn left through the gate and follow the track, which leads gently uphill. At first this will stay in woodland, and then when the track leaves the trees, the great rock tower of Y Lliwedd rises ahead.

The track enters the open hillside and you get your first glimpse of the south ridge of Snowdon. The river on the right with the waterfalls is the Afon Cwm Llan, which drains the great bowl this track leads into, the combination of Cwm Llan and Cwm Tregalan. Continue following the track, which will reach a wall just above the main **waterfall**.

Go through the gate, where there is a National Trust sign marking the entrance to the Yr Wyddfa National Nature Reserve, famous for its alpine flora. After the next track bend, the disused mine workings come into view ahead.

Past the first mine building, which is on the other side of the river from the track, you come to a weir. Just before the weir, take the eroded path on the left, which goes uphill. There is a small rock step and then the path becomes more distinct.

This path rises to meet the level track, which enters the cwm, a relic of the old mining infrastructure. The track is made level by a series of small stone viaducts. Turn right at the track to cross the viaduct and continue following the track into the cwm. The summit of Snowdon is now visible ahead.

The track crosses a slate bridge over a small stream, where the old slate mine spoil tips are visible ahead and on the right. About 200m after this bridge there is a large smoothed rocky outcrop on the left side of the path. Turn left onto the faint path that heads uphill straight after it.

The path is faint and grassy, sometimes wet. It heads directly towards Bwlch Cwm Llan, the low point on the ridge

map continues on
page 120

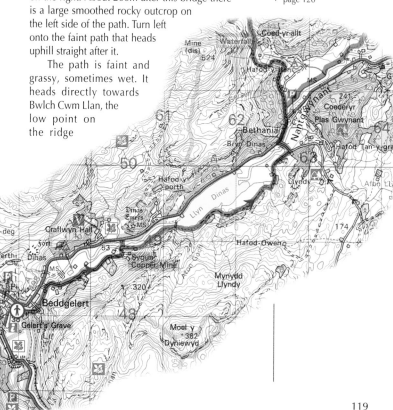

119

Cwm Llan, Snowdon's southern amphitheatre, on the much quieter side of the mountain

between Snowdon's south ridge and the slopes of Yr Aran ('the high place' or 'mountain ridge'), so if in doubt take a bearing. This path is not the right of way marked higher up on the map, but is more distinct. As it approaches Bwlch Cwm Llan, the path steepens and there are a series of stone steps.

map continues
on page 122

When the path reaches a stone wall, cross the wall and turn left, following the wall up to reach Bwlch Cwm Llan. (The small pond on the summit of the Bwlch is a good marker if the view isn't clear.) From the Bwlch,

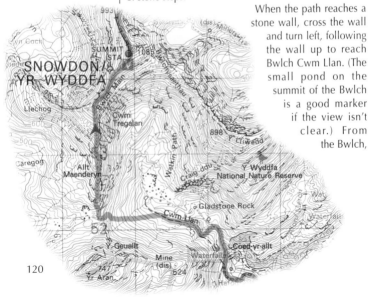

turn right, to the north, to head up the south ridge of Snowdon. The path is steep at first, with stone steps. There are a few rocky steps where hands may be needed. ▶

The south ridge is not narrow, and the path winds between the crest and the gradually sloping western side. Approximately halfway up there is a fence and a stile, and after this comes the one tricky section – a steep sloping rock face which can be difficult when wet. Either continue straight up, where you will need use of your hands, or bear to the left of the main path to avoid the scrambling section and rejoin the ridge afterwards.

Continue along the path up the south ridge, which narrows as it goes over **Bwlch Main**. There is one last steep section before it reaches the café and the summit of **Snowdon**. The summit itself is reached past the café and up a set of stone steps that will take you to the trig point, and the highest point in Wales.

The view all the way up the south ridge is spectacular on both sides, west to the Nantlle ridge and the sea, and east down into Cwm Llan.

SNOWDON

The rocks that form Snowdon are largely volcanic, created by massive eruptions around 450 million years ago in the Ordovician period. These formed two main types of rock (that are further subdivided) that can be described as those made by molten lava and magma, and those formed by the deposition of volcanic ash, which was then compressed into rock. Since then, successive ice ages have moulded the landscape into the shape we see today, and many of the most famous features on Snowdon are a result of the ice working away on the rock underneath, from the famous ridges of Y Lliwedd and Crib Goch to the deep bowls surrounding the summit on all sides. Copper and slate have both been mined on the mountain, and the ruined buildings and spoil tips are easy to spot in Cwm Llan and down the Miner's Path. Alongside the volcanic rock there is also sedimentary rock, and fossils have been found near the summit.

The presence of buildings on the summit dates back to 1838 and the railway from Llanberis was opened in 1896. Originally it was possible to stay the night in accommodation at the top, and there were several cabins available for visitors. Most of these were pulled down in the 1930s and the subsequent café lasted until 2006, when it was demolished and replaced by the current building, Hafod Eryri ('Snowdon summer house'), which was opened in 2009.

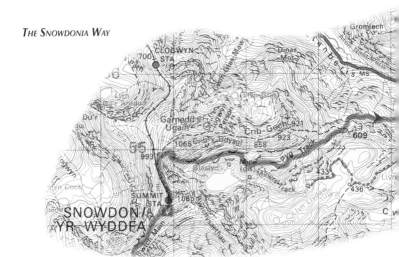

Turn right at the standing stone to descend the Pyg Track

From the summit, walk north down the track, which follows the railway line. After roughly 500 metres, at the low point of the col between Snowdon and Garnedd Ugain ('cairn of the twenty'), a large standing stone marks

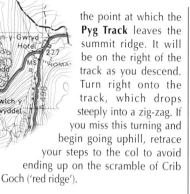

the point at which the **Pyg Track** leaves the summit ridge. It will be on the right of the track as you descend. Turn right onto the track, which drops steeply into a zig-zag. If you miss this turning and begin going uphill, retrace your steps to the col to avoid ending up on the scramble of Crib Goch ('red ridge').

Although it is now called the Pyg Track on OS maps, the true name is the **Pig Track** – a name that originates in medieval times when it would have been a route for hunting wild boar. The pass the track goes over about half an hour from Pen-y-Pass is called Bwlch y Moch, which means 'pass of the swine'.

The Pyg Track leads all the way down Snowdon to Pen-y-Pass, and although there are several rocky steps, it is mostly well defined. Llyn Glaslyn ('green lake') and Llyn Llydaw ('lakeside') are visible below the track on the right, and the steep slopes of Crib Goch tower up on the left, making this an excellent and dramatic descent. ▸

As the track approaches the knoll at 609m, towards the eastern end of **Llyn Llydaw**, there is one set of double stiles where a fence intersects the path, and shortly after this there is a left turn around a wall to continue to **Pen-y-Pass**. The trail is rocky but easy to follow.

Pen-y-Pass is the high point of the Llanberis Pass. The cluster of buildings contains a café, a National Park information centre, and across the road a YHA Hostel. Its height at 359m makes it a popular starting point for walks up Snowdon (for hostel bookings call 0845 371 9534).

Llyn Glaslyn is the source of the Afon Glaslyn, which the route followed out of Beddgelert at the beginning of the day, and which reaches the sea near Penrhyndeudraeth.

STAGE 4B
Pen-y-Pass to Capel Curig
(mountain route)

Start	Pen-y-Pass
End	Siabod Café, Capel Curig
Distance	9½ miles (15.5km)
Total ascent	4165ft (1270m)
Time	5–6hr
Terrain	Paths lead to the Bwlch y Rhediad; from here there are often no paths until the descent from Moel Siabod. The mountain ridge is broad and grassy. There is a path down to Capel Curig, and then a track in the forest.
Summits	Moel Siabod (2861ft/872m)
Maps	OS Explorer OL18 Harlech, Porthmadog & Y Bala; OS Explorer OL17 Snowdon
Supplies	Pen-y-Pass has cafés. Capel Curig has a food shop, outdoor equipment shop, cafés and a wide selection of pubs.

This stage begins by descending into the top end of Nantgwynant before climbing the side of the Moelwyns to the Bwlch y Rhediad, a pass that gives glimpses of the wild valleys to the east. The trail then follows the ridge north and east over the rocky summits of Carnedd y Cribau and Clogwyn Bwlch-y-maen before beginning the long grassy west ridge of Moel Siabod.

The view of Snowdon is probably the best from these peaks, and the narrow gap of the Llanberis Pass, with Pen-y-Pass on top, appears ominously behind you. The view from the summit of Moel Siabod is one of the most expansive in Snowdonia, with all the high mountains spread out before you, the sea on two sides and the forests of the east leading down into the Conwy Valley. Descending into Capel Curig, the trail enters the forest of Bryn Engan and crosses the Afon Llugwy before entering the village, strung out along the road like something from the Wild West.

From the **Pen-y-Pass car park**, head down the footpath on the right side of the road, which goes south-east. The path begins next to the road and goes downhill, and is initially signposted to Pen-y-Gwryd. At a path junction, turn right and downhill towards Nantgwynant. This path runs parallel to a stream and there are old farm ruins visible on the other side.

Near the bottom of the valley, the path divides again. Turn right to cross the footbridge and follow the well-made path downhill along the **Nant** map continues on page 127
Cynnyd. It leads down to **Works**, which is the site of the power station for the hydroelectric scheme leading from Llyn Llydaw on Snowdon. At the power station, turn left through a gate, up the track, which crosses the stream and heads uphill to reach a T-junction.

Turn right and go straight ahead onto the road, over a bridge to pass the farm at **Gwastadannas**. Continue along the road. Just before the farm of **Hafod Rhisgl**, the road crosses a stream. Turn left through the gate after this bridge, onto a stony path, which goes uphill.

The footpath becomes grassy and steep and leads up to the A498, where there are great views back over Llyn Gwynant ('lake in a fair valley'). From the road, the path continues uphill on the other side, slightly to the left. Immediately after leaving the

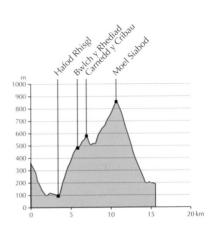

The Bwlch is a great place to look back down to the Nantgwynant, the valley at the heart of Snowdonia, and the summit of Snowdon itself.

road, take the path ahead uphill, not the one going right; soon the path enters a woodland. When the path forks in the woodland, take the right fork, which leads up. There are a few small footpath signs on this path.

The route leaves the woodland and reaches the open hillside. When it reaches a wall, ignore the metal gate and head towards the wooden stile further on. Go over this stile and follow the path bearing right uphill to reach the **Bwlch y Rhediad**. ◄

At the crest of the pass, turn left onto the faint path up the slope. There are several paths to the summit of Carnedd y Cribau, the easiest of which is to follow the fence, which crosses the hillside just after the crest of Bwlch y Rhediad but can be picked up at any time by bearing right while on the way up. At one point the fence stops at a crag but continues in the same direction beyond it.

There is a small pool next to the summit of **Carnedd y Cribau** that can be used to distinguish the summit from the other crag tops in bad weather. Following the fence will lead to this pool.

Continue following the fence down the other side of Carnedd y Cribau. There is a stile soon after; cross the stile ahead and continue north with the fence on the

right. At the next fence junction, with two stiles on the col, cross the left stile and turn right to follow the fence, aiming for the summit of **Clogwyn Bwlch-y-maen** – a rocky lump on the ridge.

Snowdon from Carnedd y Cribau

Once over this small crag, Moel Siabod ('shapely hill') is ahead. The lakes of Llynau Diwaunedd are on the right and the wide grassy ridge turns east for the ascent. A fence runs all the way up this ridge, past the shoulder of **Moel Gîd**. Ascend the ridge.

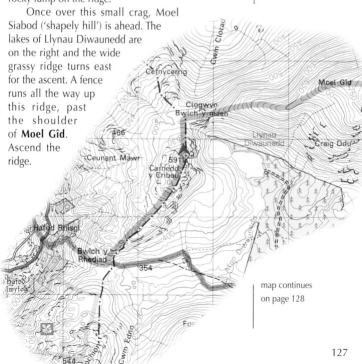

map continues
on page 128

127

When nearing the rocky debris that marks the summit area of **Moel Siabod**, there is a stile on the right. Cross this stile and continue uphill along the fence to cross another stile. Bear left to avoid the boulder field ahead, then bear right after it to rejoin the path up to the summit, which is a trig point on a rocky crown of boulders.

To descend, head north off the summit to pick up the path, after crossing another boulder-field in the direction of Capel Curig. The path is soon distinct and crosses a set of two stiles next to each other. Follow it downhill, past a boggy section where it is faint, before it becomes clear again and heads towards the woods of Bryn Engan, crossing a stile further down.

When it reaches the woods, the path runs parallel to a stream, and crosses two stiles. Just after the second stile there is a fork; go left, then left on the track and almost immediately right down a path. Follow the path

downhill, ignoring a small path on the right that shortly appears.

Looking east from the summit of Moel Siabod

The path emerges from the woods in front of **Plas y Brenin** ('hall of the king'). Turn right onto the track without crossing the river. Continue on this track past the entrance to the Plas y Brenin farm and bunkhouse, and at the track fork 500m further on from this entrance, turn left. The track leads to a bridge over the Afon Llugwy; cross it to reach the main road and arrive in **Capel Curig**, where the Siabod Café is opposite.

CAPEL CURIG ('CHAPEL OF CURIG')

Strung out for some way along the road lies the village of Capel Curig, named after the sixth-century St Curig. There is a Roman fort down the road to the east at Caer Llugwy, and many of the roads were initially built by Lord Penrhyn, owner of the Penrhyn slate works. He was also responsible for the construction of a nearby inn, which housed some of the first tourists to the area. This is now Plas y Brenin, the National Mountain Centre, which sits alongside Llynnau Mymbyr.

Capel Curig has a wide selection of accommodation, from camping to hostels to hotels. It has several pubs and cafés, and outdoor equipment shops.

STAGE 5
Dolwyddelan to Bethesda

Start	Gwydyr Hotel, Dolwyddelan
End	High Street, Bethesda
Distance	15½ miles (25.1km)
Total ascent	2165ft (660m)
Time	7–8hr
Terrain	Tracks and minor roads; some path round Llyn Ogwen
Highest point	1096ft (334m)
Maps	OS Explorer OL18 Harlech, Porthmadog & Y Bala; OS Explorer OL17 Snowdon
Supplies	Dolwyddelan has a shop and pubs; Capel Curig has cafés and a shop; Bethesda has a selection of shops.

This stage is one of the best low-level journeys through mountain terrain in the UK. It begins through forest, and then traverses the moorland round the eastern slopes of Moel Siabod. From the top of this traverse, nearly the whole of the Glyderau and Carneddau mountains are visible. You then drop down to Capel Curig before beginning the journey through the stunning Ogwen Valley.

Separating the massifs of the Glyderau and Carneddau, the valley is surrounded on all sides by giants, including the great rocky spire of Tryfan and the hulking mass of Pen yr Ole Wen. Taking you round Llyn Ogwen and continuing down the wide and peaceful expanse of the Nant Francon, the trail finishes in Bethesda, beside one of the largest slate quarries in Snowdonia.

From Gwydyr Hotel in centre of **Dolwyddelan**, near the Spar, head east down the A470. Pass a meadow on the right, and at the point where the **Afon Lledr** swings back to meet the road, turn left down the very minor road at the sign for the nursery. Once you turn onto this minor road you will see a sign saying the road is 'unsuitable for motor vehicles 250 yards ahead'.

map opposite continues on page 132

The Afon Lledr and Dolwyddelan

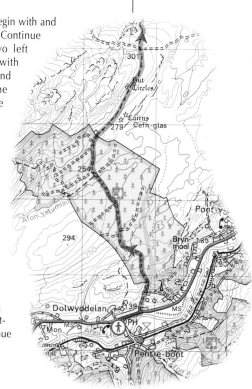

The road is steep to begin with and shortly becomes a track. Continue straight on, ignoring two left turns. At the T-junction with another track, turn left and continue ahead along the main forest track. At the next track fork, turn left, soon crossing the Afon Ystumiau, the stream that drains the southern side of Moel Siabod. Keep on the main track, ignoring side-tracks. Continue on, and the track will cross the **Afon Ystumiau** again. The impressive southern crags of Moel Siabod are visible through the trees.

About 100m after this second stream crossing there is a footpath sign pointing to Capel Curig. Continue

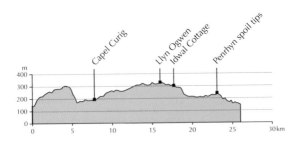

uphill and pass one more track on the left before reaching a fork. Turn right on this fork, off the main track and down a side-track. Pass through a gate and leave the forest, following the track ahead across the gorse-covered hillside.

As the track reaches the east side of Moel Siabod and arrives at the **301 spot height**, a fantastic view opens out north to the Glyderau and the Carneddau. ◄ At the next junction, keep right, ignoring the sign on the rock for the private road and the quarry.

The track now goes straight downhill, descending through a woodland. Cross the stile you come to after the

The high peak in the distance is Carnedd Llewelyn ('cairn of Llewelyn'), the third-highest mountain in England and Wales.

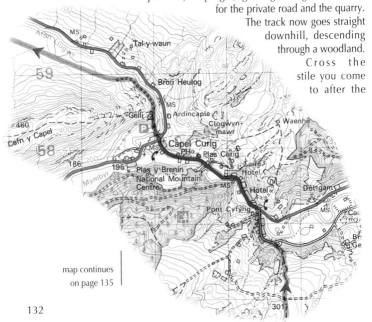

map continues
on page 135

132

track crosses a stream, follow the track to the left of a house and turn left onto the minor road. This road crosses the **Afon Llugwy** and reaches the A5. Turn left along this road and you will arrive at **Capel Curig**. There is a footpath on the side of the road all the way through.

At the junction with the **A4086**, leave the main road and go straight ahead down the minor road to the left of the Pinnacle Stores, towards the car park. Head past the car park and up the track ahead, where a footpath sign points the way to Ogwen. Look left and you will see Snowdon, with the long ridge of Y Lliwedd stretching away to the left of the summit.

The track continues ahead, past **Gelli** towards the conical summit of Pen Llithrig y Wrach before bearing left into the Ogwen valley. The view opens ahead to Pen yr Ole Wen ('head of the white slope') and Gallt yr Ogof ('hillside of the cave') as the track leads you straight on, past a National Trust sign marking the entrance into the Glyderau.

Once the track passes beneath the crags of Gallt yr Ogof, the immense rocky fin of Tryfan ('pointed mountain') comes into view on the left. The track,

Tryfan and Pen Yr Ole Wen

133

which up to now has been nearly dead straight, meets a wall and passes a small stand of trees. Pass through the gate to the campsite at **Gwern Gof Isaf** and continue along the track. Once past the house, the track reaches a crossroads. Go straight ahead, past a National Trust sign on a rock. After this sign, go onwards, ignoring the track to the hut on the left.

Cross the wooden bridge over the Nant Gwern y Gof and descend on the left of the **Gwern Gof Uchaf** campsite, house and barn. Continue ahead towards woodland. The path passes to the left of the woodland and swings right to meet the A5. Turn right, cross the road, and then almost immediately turn left down the track over the bridge.

This track leads past a house and through a small car park. Follow it over a cattle grid, and when it bends to the left you will see Llyn Ogwen ahead. The track meets a wall beside the entrance to **Tal y Llyn Ogwen** farm. Turn right up the path, cross the wall at the next stile and then take the left-hand path when it immediately splits. It will lead down towards the **lake**; follow the posts with white tops, avoiding the path that ascends to the right.

Llyn Ogwen ('lake of the lively piglet') is a glacially formed lake whose height has been raised

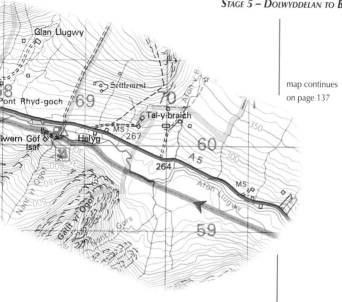

map continues
on page 137

by a dam. It is also a possible resting place of King Arthur's sword, Excalibur.

Once the path crosses a small stream via a bridge, it begins a traverse around the lake. The path is indistinct at times, but there are frequent posts to follow. From approximately halfway round, the hanging valley of Cwm Idwal in the Glyderau is visible, with the great cleft of the Devil's Kitchen surrounded by slabs and buttresses.

CWM IDWAL

A classic example of a raised valley, whose glacier would have poured into the main valley glacier of the Ogwen Valley before flowing north, Cwm Idwal is famous among climbers, botanists and geologists. The layered volcanic and sedimentary rocks visible at the back of the cwm wall have been folded up at either end – a feature known as the Idwal Syncline. On the southern side of the cwm, the exposed face of one of the layers has formed the Idwal Slabs, a climbing spot with a great range of routes.

At the back of the cwm, the rock face is split in two by the Twll Du ('black hole'), or 'Devil's Kitchen', so named by sailors travelling up the Menai Strait who would look up the valley and see cloud pouring out of the cleft. The interior of the cwm is well known for rare alpine plants, and projects nearby have sought to reduce the amount of grazing here to give the plants a better chance of survival.

The obvious remnants of the ice ages here have not always been so clear. Darwin visited and failed to see the signs, only realising on his second visit that this was full of the glacial features he had seen on his travels, and thereby helping to confirm the ice-scoured nature of the landscape.

The lake was supposedly named after Idwal, son of Owain, the 12th-century Prince of Gwynedd. Idwal was destined to become a scholar and was not suited to war, and had been sent by Owain to live with his cousin Nefydd. Nefydd became jealous as Idwal outshone his own bumbling son Dunawt and so conspired with Dunawt to get rid of Idwal. One day, walking beside the lake, Dunawt pushed Idwal in, and, unable to swim, he drowned. It is rumoured that birds do not fly over the lake because of this murderous act.

The old bridge under the new bridge at Pont Pen-y-benglog

The lakeside path leads beyond the end of the lake to where the road bridge crosses the river at **Pont Pen-y-benglog**. There are several rocky steps leading up to this point, which can be slippery. If you look down below the road bridge, you can still see the old bridge, the stones suspended between the rocky banks of the river.

On the road, turn left to reach Ogwen Cottage, admiring the waterfall of **Rhaeadr Ogwen** ('waterfall of the lively piglet') on the far side of the bridge. Turn right here off the main road through the car park and past the Idwal Cottage YHA. Continue along a small road straight ahead through the trees, which leads into the **Nant Ffrancon** ('valley or stream of the soldier'). ▶

This road bends right as it descends through the valley, and the great spoil tips of the Penrhyn Quarries appear ahead. Continue following the road for several kilometres until it bends right to cross the river, and then, at the point at which it bends, follow the cycle track straight ahead through the gate. It heads towards the spoil tips and reaches their foot, traversing right beneath them.

The track heads down to the river. Continue on the left side of the river and do not cross the bridge. At the next road after passing this bridge, cross straight over to

The Nant Ffrancon is a textbook example of a glacial U-shaped valley, gouged out by ice over tens of thousands of years.

map continues on page 138

137

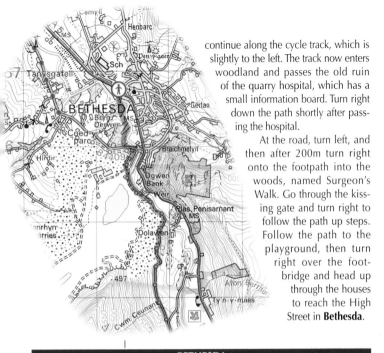

continue along the cycle track, which is slightly to the left. The track now enters woodland and passes the old ruin of the quarry hospital, which has a small information board. Turn right down the path shortly after passing the hospital.

At the road, turn left, and then after 200m turn right onto the footpath into the woods, named Surgeon's Walk. Go through the kissing gate and turn right to follow the path up steps. Follow the path to the playground, then turn right over the footbridge and head up through the houses to reach the High Street in **Bethesda**.

BETHESDA

At the end of the Ogwen Valley lies Bethesda. Named after the chapel first established here at the beginning of the 19th century, the name is biblical and has no translation into English. The main industry that caused the growth of the town was the colossal Penrhyn slate works on the northern slopes of the Glyderau, which hang above the town. Full-scale extraction started in the 1780s, and at its height during the 19th century this was the largest slate quarry in the world, and the deepest man-made hole on earth.

Unfortunately for workers and owners, the other record it broke was for the longest industrial dispute in British history, when there was a three-year lockout from 1900 to 1903 by workers demanding better pay and safer working conditions. Although it now has a much reduced workforce than in its heyday, the quarry is still in operation and is owned by Welsh Slate Ltd.

Also on site is a mile-long zip wire run by Zip World, which gives you a unique view of the quarry below! Zip World run tours of the quarry as well as the zip wire (tel 01248 601444, www.zipworld.co.uk).

STAGE 5A

Capel Curig to Bethesda
(mountain route)

Start	A5/A4086 junction, Capel Curig
End	High street, Bethesda
Distance	12¾ miles (20.4km)
Total ascent	5380ft (1640m)
Time	7–8hr
Terrain	High mountain terrain; sometimes paths
Summits	Y Foel Goch (2641ft/805m), Glyder Fach (3261ft/994m), Glyder Fawr (3284ft/1001m), Y Garn (3107ft/947m), Mynydd Perfedd (2664ft/812m), Carnedd y Filiast (2693ft/821m)
Maps	OS Explorer OL17 Snowdon
Supplies	Capel Curig and Bethesda have a few shops, cafés and pubs.

This truly epic mountain journey takes in the whole of the Glyderau ridge. Staying above 700m nearly all the way from Capel Curig to Bethesda, it begins with the long ascent up to the bouldery summit of Glyder Fach. The ridge is easy to follow and the paths are good. Snowdon is on the left and the Carneddau on the right, with the plunging depths of the Ogwen Valley in-between.

From Glyder Fach, the route crosses a rocky plateau, taking you among the pinnacles marking the summit area of Glyder Fawr and then turning north towards the pointed peak of Y Garn. Rougher terrain is then encountered up over Mynydd Perfedd to Carnedd y Filiast, where Anglesey and the Menai Strait are visible ahead. The final drop down into the Nant Ffrancon is steep but there is a faint path; once in the valley, the route heads into Bethesda, past the looming remains of the Penrhyn slate quarry.

From the road junction of the A5 and A4086 in **Capel Curig**, go up the road to the left of the Pinnacle Stores towards the car park. Cross the bridge, go past the car

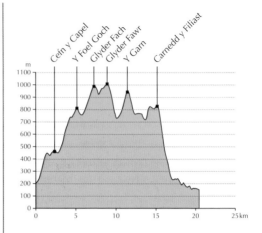

park and continue over the cattle grid. Follow the track to **Gelli**.

Cross the stile at Gelli and turn left onto a path. After 20m, at the junction, do not continue left following the fence past the house. Instead, continue straight ahead, crossing the path. The path ahead is hidden by under-growth but is clear once you're on it. It starts by running

map continues on page 143

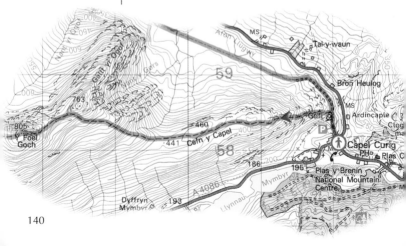

above the house, then bears right uphill. It is indistinct from here, so keep aiming for the left-hand side of the central rocky pinnacle ahead.

The path heads up the left side of the ridge before moving to the crest to reach the east top of Cefn y Capel, where there is a view ahead to Gallt yr Ogof ('hillside of the cave') and Y Foel Goch ('the bald red hill'). Continue along the ridge to the **Cefn y Capel** summit.

Descend to the boggy col and then begin the ascent of Gallt yr Ogof. The path skirts to the south side of the summit and rejoins the ridge at the col before Y Foel Goch. Tryfan ('pointed mountain'), Glyder Fach ('little heap') and Y Garn ('the cairn') are all now visible.

From the summit of **Y Foel Goch**, descend to **Llyn Caseg-fraith**, being careful not to follow the paths off to the left down to the Pen-y-Gwryd. After passing the lake, continue up the rocky slopes of **Glyder Fach**. Near the top the path enters a boulder field where you should pick your own route. Small piles of stones mark a faint path but there are easier and harder ways of clambering over the boulders and sometimes the most direct way is the most fun.

The rock-strewn summit of Glyder Fach

141

The famous Cantilever Stone

The summit area is a plateau that feels like a moonscape. The summit itself is the peak of a large pile of boulders over on the western side of the plateau. ◄

Head west from the summit to the left of the spectacular rocky crown of Castell y Gwynt ('castle of the winds'). The path passes through a small boulder field and then becomes distinct from **Bwlch y Ddwy Glyder**. Avoid the paths leading right, which descend Y Gribin.

Look out for the famous rock feature of the Cantilever Stone – a jutting flat boulder suspended like a diving board.

The path disintegrates on the way up to **Glyder Fawr** ('big heap') but a series of cairns mark the way to the rocky pinnacles the mark the summit.

THE GLYDERAU

The long ridge stretching from Capel Curig to Bethesda is made up of a group of peaks collectively known as the Glyderau, or anglicised to 'The Glyders'. They are named after the two highest peaks, Glyder Fawr and Glyder Fach, and the collective name Glyderau is thought to originate from the Welsh *cludair*, meaning a heap of stones. As well as the two Glyders, they contain three other peaks above 3000 feet.

As is typical on British mountains, their western and southern sides are smoother and less steep than those to the north and east. This is due to our prevailing weather coming from the south-west, meaning that the glaciers of the ice ages were more likely to build up on the colder and more sheltered northern and eastern sides, where they also took longer to melt. Today this can be seen in the impressive cwms of Tryfan, Bochlwyd and Idwal, and glacial action is also the reason for the formation of lakes in many of these features.

The Glyderau are home to two enormous slate quarries, at Penrhyn and Dinorwig. The Dinorwig quarry above Llanberis is now the site of a hydro-electric pumped storage system that has earned it the name 'the electric mountain', and the old quarry walls are famous among climbers.

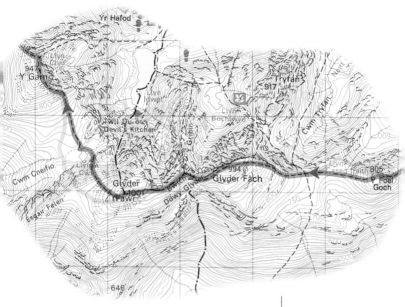

Descend west towards Y Garn; cairns lead the way to a steep and stony zig-zag path that descends to **Llyn y Cŵn** ('lake of the dogs'). The path passes by the lake, to its north side, crossing the stream that drains it, and

map continues on page 145

The south ridge of Y Garn and Tryfan

143

then bears right just afterwards to head towards Y Garn.

After a few hundred metres there is another fork in the path. Both routes lead to the summit but the right fork is a more interesting and easier route, heading up to the ridge and then turning left towards the summit. ◄

From the ridge walk there is a great view down to Llyn Clyd, which you do not get from the other path.

From the summit of **Y Garn** descend north-north-west to the col, where the path forks. Take the left path, which contours around **Foel Goch** and rejoins the ridge at **Bwlch y Brecan**. After this bwlch, as the path bears left to ascend Elidir Fawr, take the path on the right, which runs parallel to the fence and runs steeply up the side of **Mynydd Perfedd**.

At the top of the slope, cross the stile on the right to reach the summit, then head north on a wide ridge towards **Carnedd y Filiast**. Cross a stile over a stone wall to reach the top, which is a mass of boulders with a steep drop on the other side that makes it feel like a small rocky ridge.

To descend, turn north-east and follow the bouldery summit ridge towards Bethesda, which can be seen in the valley below. A faint path soon begins on the right side of the boulder field. Once past the boulders the ridge path becomes clear and aims for the cluster of houses at Ty'n-y-maes ('house of the meadow').

The path becomes fainter as the slope becomes less steep. Head straight down, keeping just to the left of the rocky outcrops. When the slope drops off steeply again ahead, the path turns left to run along the top of this drop, towards the stream in **Cwm Ceunant**.

When the slope below eases off, the path bears right diagonally down and crosses the first of two streams,

which run almost parallel to each other. The path then descends between these streams. Cross the second stream near the fence and head left to a gate that opens onto a track. Once on the track, turn left.

The track winds its way underneath the slate spoil tips of Penrhyn Quarry and soon runs alongside the river. Continue on the left side of the river and do not cross the bridge. At the next road after passing this bridge, cross straight over to continue along the cycle track, which is slightly to the left. The track now enters woodland and passes the old ruin of the quarry hospital, which has a small information board. Turn right down the path shortly after passing the hospital.

At the road, turn left, and then after 200m turn right onto the footpath into the woods, named Surgeon's Walk. Go through the kissing gate and turn right to follow the path up steps. Follow the path to the playground, then turn right over the footbridge and head up through the houses to reach the High Street in **Bethesda**.

STAGE 6
Bethesda to Conwy

Start	War memorial, Bethesda
End	Rosemary Lane, Conwy
Distance	21 miles (33.6km)
Total ascent	4855ft (1480m)
Time	10–11hr
Terrain	Grassy upland paths and tracks, with some small road sections
Highest point	1286ft (392m)
Maps	OS Explorer OL17 Snowdon
Supplies	Bethesda, Llanfairfechan and Conwy have a selection of shops, pubs and cafés.
Note	This is by far the longest of the low-level stages, with sections of relatively remote paths that are definitely 'in the hills' rather than the valleys. If you have any doubts about your fitness for this stage, consider splitting it up at Llanfairfechan and spending the night there before continuing.

The final stage takes you along the flanks of the Carneddau Mountains – the largest area of high ground in England and Wales. The route crosses the northern slopes, with views over the Menai Strait, Anglesey and the Irish Sea. You cross high moorland, take an inland detour to visit the spectacular Aber Falls, and finish with a panoramic descent into Conwy where on a clear day you can see the Arans far away to the south, near where you started the Snowdonia Way. Although the day is long and includes a few ascents, much of the distance is taken up along level upland tracks.

From the war memorial on **Bethesda**'s High Street (also the A5), go west past the Spar and turn right to follow the road Allt Pen y Bryn uphill (signposted for the school). Turn left at the roundabout, still following signs for the school. Pass the school on your right; turn right down the next

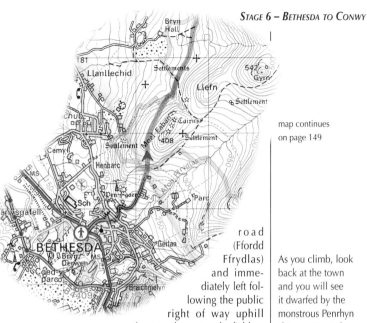

map continues
on page 149

road
(Ffordd
Ffrydlas)
and imme-
diately left fol-
lowing the public
right of way uphill
between houses and a field.

This path reaches a road; turn right and then left up Cilfodan, a single-lane road leading out of Bethesda. ▶

The road becomes a track; continue uphill through a gate and into a field, keeping to the right of the wall. Pass through another gate to the open moor. There are now several paths; take the one heading directly ahead, aiming for the summit of Moel Faban. Cross a small stream and shortly come to a junction of grassy paths. Turn left, walk only 10m or so, and look out for a path that appears on your right. It will be indistinct at first but then becomes clear. Take this path, which passes to the left of **Moel Faban** across hillsides of scrubby gorse. ▶

At the next path fork, take the left option, which goes slightly downhill. This reaches a rough track, which soon becomes a grassy path. Continue in the same direction, at roughly the same height. This path leads over 2km across the hillside; continue along it in a straight line, avoiding

As you climb, look back at the town and you will see it dwarfed by the monstrous Penrhyn slate quarry and the mountains of the Glyderau.

The Menai Strait, Anglesey and Puffin Island soon appear – a spectacular view that dominates for much of the day.

147

The 37m-high Aber Falls is one of the highlights of Stage 6

other faint paths leading up or downhill. At times the path is faint, but persist!

At a fork roughly 20m away from a slate fence on the left, take the right fork. This path will naturally lead gently down to a wall with a metal ladder over it. Cross the wall, descend through a field to a track. Turn right onto the track.

This track contours along the hillside, through fields as it heads towards the valley containing the Afon Rhaeadr-fawr ('river of the big waterfall'). To the left, if the tide is out, you will be able to see the mudflat of the Lavan Sands. The track swings right to enter the valley from high up, turning south. Mountains appear ahead and on the right, the most prominent being Llwytmor ('upper grey sea') with forest plantations crowding its lower slopes. ▶

The impressive Aber Falls is visible at the head of the valley.

The track continues through more fields, passing to the left of a small forest, and heads gradually downhill. At a gate, turn right round a small stand of trees to cross a stream. A path appears on the left, supported by a footpath sign. Take this path, which leads down towards the **Afon Gam**, which it crosses.

The path bears left under steep slopes and crosses the **Afon Rhaeadr-bach** ('river of the small waterfall') via a footbridge before reaching the **Afon Rhaeadr-fawr**, and the 37m-high waterfall of **Aber Falls**. Cross the bridge and turn left, following the well-maintained gravelled

map continues on page 150

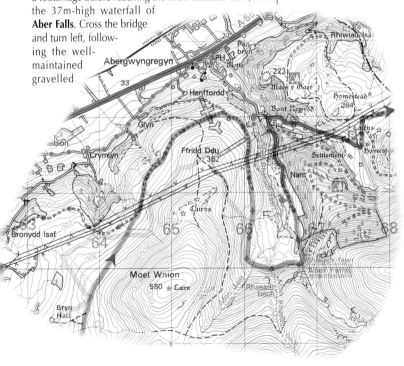

map continues on
page 152

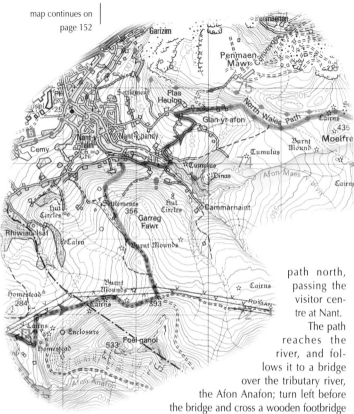

path north, passing the visitor centre at Nant.

The path reaches the river, and follows it to a bridge over the tributary river, the Afon Anafon; turn left before the bridge and cross a wooden footbridge over the Afon Rhaeadr-fawr, following the path on the right until it reaches the road bridge. Cross the road bridge back over the Afon Rhaedr-fawr. After the bridge, keep straight ahead along the road that goes uphill.

At this point you are walking along a Roman road, built to subdue the natives after the invasion.

At the end of the road pass through the small car park and bear right to go through the gate on the far side. A track leads uphill, soon turning left past the National Trust sign for the Carneddau and bearing right when it passes between the power lines. ◄

The **Carneddau mountains** occupy 10% of the area of the National Park, have seven summits over 3000ft, and are an area of wild beauty. There is evidence of human habitation going back thousands of years, and there are over 1000 ancient sites documented in and around these mountains.

Heading up into the northern Carneddau

This track leads up to the spot height at **393**; continue for 50m and then turn left (there is a signpost) towards Llanfairfechan ('lesser church of St Mary's'). Follow the track, and several footpath signs, along the first top and left downhill past the summit of **Garreg Fawr**. After following a wall for a short time, there are three paths heading away down the slope in front.

Take the central path, which bears slightly right of your previous direction and points directly at Puffin Island. At a path fork, go left. Upon reaching a wall, pass through the gate and bear right, steeply down through gorse, ignoring a left turn, and then through a gate to pass between fences that border fields and houses.

Descend to the road in **Nant y pandy**, on the outskirts of Llanfairfechan.

TO SPLIT THE STAGE AT LLANFAIRFECHAN

Walkers who want to stopover at Llanfairfechan should turn left on the road and then right after 50m, down stone steps. At the road, turn right to cross the bridge and then left at the next road. Follow this road to reach the town centre.

To continue on the route, turn right at the road, which ascends gently uphill then downhill to the river. Ignore the road with the 'dead end' sign that lies straight ahead as the road bends left. Cross the river and turn right along Newry Drive. The road zig-zags up past a nature reserve. Continue along it until it reaches the T-junction and the sign for Waen Farm. Turn left and take the next road on your right, after a few hundred metres.

At the turning circle at the end of the road, continue straight ahead through the gate onto a track. This track passes between farm buildings and soon becomes a path to the upper moor; when it leaves the farm, follow the fence. The path swings right and ascends; on reaching two gates next to each other, go through the left one and continue ahead, following the fence.

When the fence ends, pass through the gate and continue straight ahead. The path leads towards **Moelfre** ('bare hill') and then heads for its left-hand side.

You are now in some fantastically bleak moorland. On the right side the land rises to the jumbled rocky peak of **Tal y Fan**, although

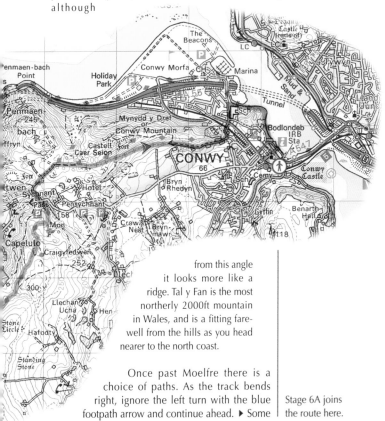

from this angle it looks more like a ridge. Tal y Fan is the most northerly 2000ft mountain in Wales, and is a fitting farewell from the hills as you head nearer to the north coast.

Once past Moelfre there is a choice of paths. As the track bends right, ignore the left turn with the blue footpath arrow and continue ahead. ▶ Some

Stage 6A joins the route here.

50m after this there is a track fork; go left, and then at the path fork immediately afterwards, take the right option, which is more like straight ahead. This path leads you gently contouring across the slope, and then up to a stone circle. Continue past the first circle and follow the path to reach an even bigger stone circle.

Continue along the path in the same direction past the second stone circle and follow it downhill to rejoin the track. Turn right on the track and follow it up and over a col, and then downhill on the other side, under some power lines, where there is a wall on the right.

As the house at **Bryn Dawydd** comes into view, the track bends right through a gate. Descend with it and then follow it as it turns left along the line of trees and past the house, passing through a gate soon afterwards.

After this gate, continue ahead following the wall and look out for a right-hand turn through a black gate, towards a green hut, where there is a signpost. The path heads towards the hut, then bears right before it and crosses the bridge over the **Afon Gyrach**. Continue straight up the other side to a wall corner. Follow the wall uphill for around 100m, roughly halfway up the slope. A path will appear on the left, which is signposted. Follow this grassy path, which leads you round the hillside.

Conwy Mountain is now visible ahead, and a giant offshore wind farm in the distance.

The track reaches and runs next to a wall, before swinging right, away from it, to reach a fork of tracks. Turn left and follow this track up until it reaches the wall of the Pensychnant Nature Reserve and Farm, where the track swings right. Cross the stile ahead and follow the path through the nature reserve, taking the left path when it forks. At the next path junction, turn left. ◄

The path descends to a small forest; turn left, and shortly reach the **Sychnant Pass**. Cross the road and head up the gravelled track on the other side of the pass. This track continues for 200m before bearing right and then left. Turn right onto the stony uphill track at the junction after this left bend.

At the next junction, where there is a marshy pond on the right, turn right onto the track. You have now begun the final descent of the Snowdonia Way. Soon

Conwy Castle will come into view, surrounded by the town of Conwy and facing the town of Llandudno over the mouth of the Afon Conwy ('full and flowing river').

After two small rises, this track descends in a roughly straight line down to Conwy. At the only path junction, continue ahead in the same direction, downhill. The track eventually becomes Mountain Road at a small lay-by. Take a left at the first road junction after this, onto what is still Mountain Road, past the sign for Beechwood Court. Continue down the track straight ahead and cross the footbridge over the **railway**.

At the crossroads after the footbridge, continue straight ahead over the road, keeping the school on the right. Take the first right after the school, following the tarmac track along the banks of the Afon Conwy to reach the **Conwy** waterfront and the **castle**. From the waterfront, pass through the arch and head up Lower Gate Street, next to the Liverpool Arms. This road becomes High Street and heads up to reach Lancaster Square. The Snowdonia Way ends at the first signpost in Rosemary Lane, just past Lancaster Square and next to the entrance to the **train station**.

CONWY

Conwy Castle and the Afon Conwy

Standing near the mouth of the Afon Conwy, this impressive town is dominated by the castle, built in the late 13th century by Edward I as part of his conquest of Wales. It was designed to dominate the landscape and put an end to Welsh resistance to the English crown, which tells us as much about the persistence of the Welsh princes as it does about English might.

Surrounding the town are the original stone walls, built at the same time, and in an impressively complete state. There are 22 towers, and several access points where you can walk round the ramparts, nearly circumnavigating the town from above. Part of the wall incorporated Llewellyn the Great's *llys* (court house), which can still be identified by the windows in the outer wall.

Besides these impressive medieval structures, you can also visit the 14th-century merchant's house at Aberconwy House, the Elizabethan townhouse at Plas Mawr, and even Britain's smallest house, which stands on the waterfront. Opposite the castle is the suspension bridge built by Thomas Telford, which is now only open to pedestrians. There is a visitor centre near the train station.

Conwy Castle is open all year except a few days around Christmas: April to October 9am–5pm, November to March 9.30am–4pm Mon–Sat and 11am–4pm Sun (www.conwy-castle.co.uk).

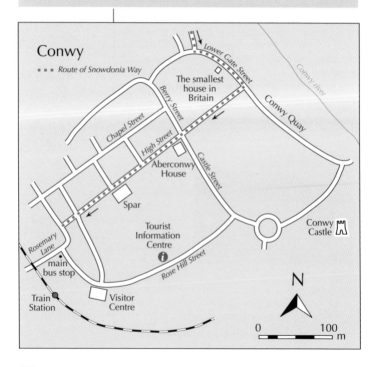

STAGE 6A

Bethesda to Conwy
(mountain route)

Start	War memorial, Bethesda
End	Rosemary Lane, Conwy
Distance	18 miles (28.7km)
Total ascent	5216ft (1590m)
Time	9–10hr
Terrain	Upland paths and open mountainside
Summits	Carnedd Gwenllian (3038ft/926m), Foel-fras (3090ft/942m), Drum (2526ft/770m)
Maps	OS Explorer OL17 Snowdon
Supplies	Bethesda and Conwy have a selection of shops, pubs and cafés.

The crossing of the Carneddau is the most remote section of the mountain route and gives a real sense of the vastness of this part of Snowdonia. Leaving Bethesda, the trail quickly enters the hills and climbs up the magnificent route to Carnedd Gwenllian, where the great peaks of Yr Elen and Carnedd Llewelyn rear their craggy bulks ahead. The route then turns north-east and traverses the wide and grassy ridge all the way to the Roman road at the Bwlch y Ddeufaen.

With the sea and Great Orme's Head now visible ahead, the path crosses the open moor north of Tal y Fan before beginning the long and gentle descent down to Conwy, via the dramatic Sychnant Pass and the heathland of Conwy Mountain. Conwy itself lies on the near side of the great Afon Conwy, with the brooding castle dominating the view of the town.

From the war memorial on **Bethesda**'s High Street (also the A5), go west past the Spar and turn right to follow the road Allt Pen y Bryn uphill (signposted for the school). Turn left at the roundabout, still following signs for the school. Pass the school on your right; turn right down the next road (Ffordd Ffrydlas) and immediately left following the public right of way uphill between houses and a field.

map continues on
page 160

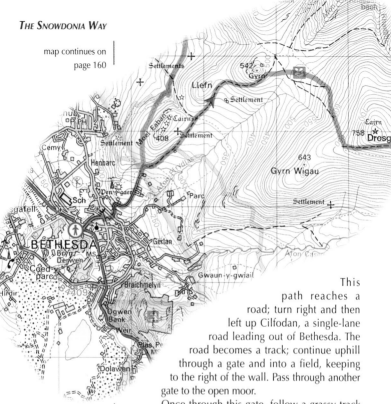

This path reaches a road; turn right and then left up Cilfodan, a single-lane road leading out of Bethesda. The road becomes a track; continue uphill through a gate and into a field, keeping to the right of the wall. Pass through another gate to the open moor.

Once through this gate, follow a grassy track which bears right at first before bending left and heading up the valley containing the Afon Ffrydlas. The pointed rocky summit of Gryn is soon visible ahead.

At a fork in the track, follow the route on the left, and at the next fork as the track approaches **Llefn**, take the one on the right. There are now faint paths on both sides, but continue towards Gryn. The path leads towards the left side of Gryn but before passing it, bears right to pass under **Gryn** and then left to lead up to the col. There is a faint path fork before the col; at this fork go right.

The col is wide and flat, a good first taster of the Carneddau you are entering. The path here is not distinct, but head towards Drosgl. Continue up the slope and

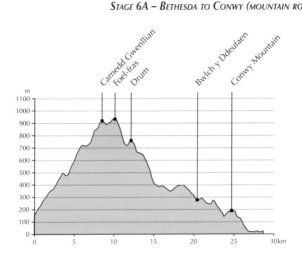

eventually the path becomes clear, leading uphill and bearing slightly right.

Follow this path as it gradually bends left up to the col between Drosgl and Gyrn Wigau; it is well defined and stony. On the col, at a small pile of stones, the path forks. Take the left path uphill. The path soon bears right and contours round the slope of **Drosgl** to the col before Bera Bach. Sometimes this path feels more like a grassy vehicle track. ▶

On this col just before **Bera Bach** the path divides; take the right-hand route, which traverses to the right of

From the col there is an excellent view into the northern cwms of the Carneddau, with the great mass of Carnedd Llewelyn ('cairn of Llewelyn [the Great]') dominating the landscape.

THE CARNEDDAU

The Carneddau cover 10% of Snowdonia, and stretch from the sea in the north, to the Ogwen Valley in the south and west, and the Afon Conwy in the east.

Meaning 'the cairns', this most northerly of Wales' mountain ranges is the highest continuous area of land in England and Wales, with seven peaks above 3000 feet. The area is covered with ancient monuments, the most numerous being the cairns themselves, Bronze Age burial chambers located on many prominent points, and on the highest summits in the area, Carnedd Llewelyn and Carnedd Dafydd. There are also numerous standing stones, stone circles, and the remains of settlements, which you can try and identify as you pass them by.

Most of the mountainsides are cloaked in grass and, in the damper places, soft-rush. There are also areas of heather, and woodlands in the valleys, but many of the higher slopes can be quite monotonous for plant life. Alongside sheep, you are quite likely to see the wild ponies that are free to roam over these hills, and perhaps a feral goat or two.

Bera Bach, beneath the boulder-strewn slopes on the southern side. The path can be faint, and bends left to rise up the slope after passing the rocky debris, staying on the south side of the ridge.

map continues on page 162

About 500m past Bera Bach there is a faint Y-junction in the path, which is marked by two small clusters of stones 5m apart. Take the left-hand path. (If this junction is missed, or there are doubts about the path, simply head up towards the rocky outcrop of Yr Aryg.)

The path passes to the right of the **Yr Aryg** boulder field and heads up onto a broad slope. When it reaches the crest of the slope and Foel-fras ('broad

hill') appears ahead, bear right at the indistinct path crossroads to reach the summit of **Carnedd Gwenllian**, over a rocky summit slope. (If you lose the path, take a bearing for the summit of Carnedd Gwenllian.)

The summit of Carnedd Gwenllian

> Formerly known as Carnedd Uchaf, **Carnedd Gwenllian** was renamed in 2009 to honour Princess Gwenllian, the only daughter of Llewelyn ap Gruffudd, the last native prince of Wales. Gruffudd was killed in battle shortly before Edward I began his invasion of North Wales. Gwenllian was allowed to live, but spent the rest of her life hidden in a priory in Lincolnshire, where she died aged 55.

The top of Carnedd Gwenllian is a bouldery plateau with a cluster of large boulders forming the summit. If visibility is poor, make sure you have not mistaken the similar rocky outcrop at Yr Aryg for the summit. To check, simply head a bit further south-east. If you're on the true summit, the slope will drop away downhill, but if you're at Yr Aryg, it will be flat and then continue uphill.

map continues on
page 164

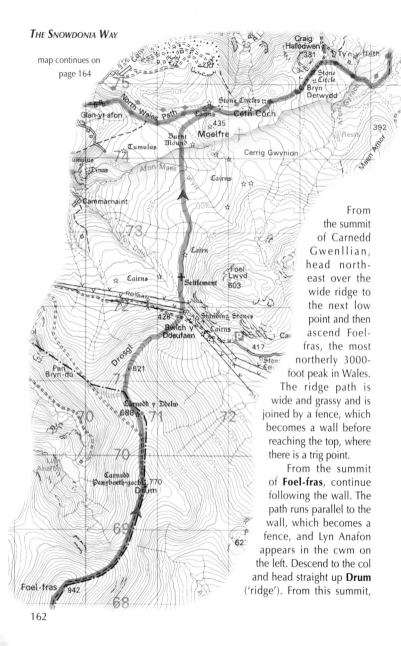

From the summit of Carnedd Gwenllian, head north-east over the wide ridge to the next low point and then ascend Foel-fras, the most northerly 3000-foot peak in Wales. The ridge path is wide and grassy and is joined by a fence, which becomes a wall before reaching the top, where there is a trig point.

From the summit of **Foel-fras**, continue following the wall. The path runs parallel to the wall, which becomes a fence, and Lyn Anafon appears in the cwm on the left. Descend to the col and head straight up **Drum** ('ridge'). From this summit,

The northern slopes of the Carneddau, including the reservoir of Llyn Anafon

descend along the track, which slowly bends left as it descends.

After a few hundred metres, turn right onto the path marked by a pile of stones just off the track on the right. This path leads to the north-west end of **Carnedd y Ddelw** and joins the fence on the summit ridge. Follow the fence, and turn right when it turns right, downhill, on a path that leads down to **Bwlch y Ddeufaen** and the track of the Roman road. ▶

Cross the track and follow the path ahead, bearing left at the fork and following the grassy path as it contours round the base of Foel Lwyd. At the next Y-junction, where there is a large flat-faced boulder ahead and slightly to the left, take the right fork. The path continues to a crossroads of paths, at which you should continue straight on.

About 200m further on, at a Y-junction, go right, and then shortly after this at the next Y-junction, go right again. (These junctions are faint and grassy; if in doubt, aim for the left-hand side of Moelfre, the grassy hill ahead across the marsh.) At the first stream reached, take the right path afterwards to cross more marshy ground. The path begins

Bwlch y Ddeufaen means the 'pass of the two stones', and slightly down the track on the right side of the pass the two standing stones are still there.

163

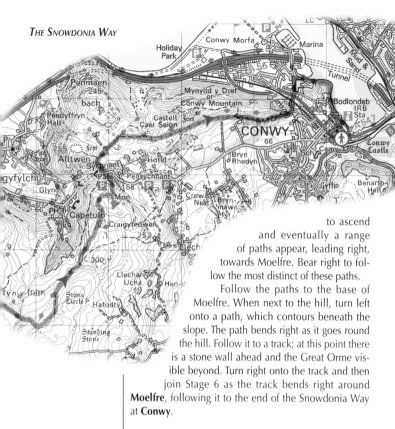

to ascend and eventually a range of paths appear, leading right, towards Moelfre. Bear right to follow the most distinct of these paths.

Follow the paths to the base of Moelfre. When next to the hill, turn left onto a path, which contours beneath the slope. The path bends right as it goes round the hill. Follow it to a track; at this point there is a stone wall ahead and the Great Orme visible beyond. Turn right onto the track and then join Stage 6 as the track bends right around **Moelfre**, following it to the end of the Snowdonia Way at **Conwy**.

APPENDIX A

Accommodation

An internet search will yield further options for most of the places listed below; these are just a selection of the various types of accommodation available in and near each of the stages.

Machynlleth

Campsite
Gwerniago (in Pennal, 3 miles west of Machynlleth)
tel 01654 791227
contact@gwerniago.co.uk
www.gwerniago.co.uk

Hostel
Corris Hostel (in Corris, 6 miles north of Machynlleth)
tel 01654 761686
mail@corrishostel.co.uk
www.corrishostel.co.uk

B&Bs/guest houses
Dyfiview
tel 01654 702023
nfo@dyfiview.co.uk
www.dyfiview.co.uk

Maenllwyd
tel 01654 702928
maenllwyd@btinternet.com
www.maenllwyd.co.uk

Hotel
The White Lion
tel 01654 703455
enquiries@whitelionhotel.co.uk
www.whitelionhotel.co.uk

Abergynolwyn

There is very little accommodation in the village.

Campsite
Cedris Farm (1 mile north-east of the village)
tel 01654 782280
brynllinos@hotmail.com
ffermcedrisfarm.wales

B&Bs/guest houses
Riverside Guest House
tel 01654 782235

The Dolgoch (2½ miles south-west of the village)
tel 01654 782258

The Old Rectory on the Lake (2½ miles north-east of the village)
tel 01654 782225
enquiries@rectoryonthelake.co.uk
www.rectoryonthelake.co.uk

Hotel
Ty'n y Cornel (2½ miles north-east of the village)
tel 01654 782282
www.tynycornel.co.uk

Dolgellau

Campsite
Tal-y-Fron (campsite with camping cabins)
tel 01341 422638
info@tal-y-fron.co.uk
www.campsitesnowdonia.co.uk

B&Bs/guest houses
Aber Cottage
tel 01341 421413
abercottage@btinternet.com
www.abercottage.com

Ty Seren
tel 01341 423407
enquiries@ty-serenbandb.co.uk
www.ty-serenbandb.co.uk

Hotel
The Royal Ship
tel 01341 422209
info@royalship.pub
www.robinsonsbrewery.com/
royalshiphotel

Trawsfynydd

Campsite
Cae Adda (campsite with camping
cabin, 30min walk from village)
tel 01766 540441
caeaddacamping@aol.co.uk
www.caeadda.com

Hostels
Llys Ednowain
tel 01766 770324
llysednowain@btconnect.com

Treks Bunkhouse (6 miles to the north,
near Ffestiniog)
tel 07796 172318
treksbunkhouse@gmail.com
www.treksbunkhouse.co.uk

B&B/guest house
Old Mill Farmhouse
tel 01766 540397
stay@oldmillfarmhouse.co.uk
www.oldmillfarmhouse.co.uk

Hotel
Cross Foxes
tel 01766 540232

Penrhyndeudraeth

Campsite
Blaen Cefn Leisure Park (1 mile outside
town)
tel 01766 770014
www.blaencefnleisure.co.uk

B&B/guest house
There are plenty of hotels and B&Bs in
and around Porthmadog, a short bus/
train journey west of Penrhyndeudraeth.

Wenallt
tel 01766 770321
i.hartill@btinternet.com
www.wenalltguesthouse.co.uk

Beddgelert

Campsite
Cae Du
tel 01766 890345
www.caeducampsite.co.uk

Hostel
YHA Bryn Gwynant (4 miles north-east
of the village)
tel 0845 3719108
www.yha.org.uk

B&Bs/guest houses
Plas Gwyn
tel 01766 890215
stay@plas-gwyn.com
www.plas-gwyn.com

Colwyn Guest House
tel 01766 890276
colwynguesthouse@tiscali.co.uk
www.beddgelertguesthouse.co.uk

Hotel
The Royal Goat
tel 01766 890224
info@royalgoathotel.co.uk
www.royalgoathotel.co.uk

Pen-y-Pass
The only place to stay at Pen-y-Pass is
the hostel:
YHA Snowdon Pen-y-Pass
tel 0845 3719534
penypass@yha.org.uk
www.yha.org.uk

A short bus journey or a 30-minute
walk down the path that goes initially
south-east takes you to

Pen-y-Gwryd Hotel
tel 01286 870211
escape@pyg.co.uk
www.pyg.co.uk

Alternatively, there are buses north-
west to Llanberis or north-east to
Capel Curig where there are several
choices of hotels, B&Bs, hostels and
campsites.

Dolwyddelan

Campsite
Bryn Tirion
tel 01690 750366
price768@btinternet.com

Hostel
Lledr House (1 mile down the road in
the village of Pont-y-Pant)
tel 01690 750202
lledrhouse@aol.com
lledrhouse.co.uk

Hotel
There is a wide range of hotels and
B&Bs in Betws-y-Coed, which is a
10-minute train/bus/taxi journey from
Dolwyddelan.

Elen's Castle (including a small
bunkhouse)
tel 01690 750207
stay@hotelinsnowdonia.co.uk
www.hotelinsnowdonia.co.uk

Capel Curig

Campsite and bunkhouse
Bryn Trych Farm
tel 01690 720414
www.heartofsnowdonia.co.uk/btfcamp.
htm

Hostel
Plas Curig
tel 01690 720225
info@snowdoniahostel.co.uk
snowdoniahostel.co.uk

Hotel
Tyn y Coed
tel 01690 720331
www.tyn-y-coed.co.uk

Bethesda

Bunkhouses
Tyddyn Du (groups of 6 or more)
www.bunkhouse-tyddyndu.co.uk

Victoria Bunkhouse
tel 01248 600997
victoriabunkhouse@hotmail.co.uk
www.victoriabunkhouse.co.uk

B&B/guest house
There is a wide range of
accommodation in Bangor, which

is a 30-minute bus journey north of Bethesda. Alternatively, the Idwal Cottage YHA is 4½ miles south, although at the time of writing there is no bus that way.

Joys of Life Country Park
tel 01248 602122
enquiries@thejoysoflife.co.uk
www.thejoysoflife.co.uk

Llanfairfechan

Campsite and bunkhouse
Platt's Farm
tel 01248 680105
sam@plattsfarm.com
www.plattsfarm.com

B&Bs/guest houses
Min y Don
tel 01248 680742
minydon1@aol.com
www.min-y-don.co.uk

Y Gelli
tel 01248 680643
welcome@y-gelli.co.uk
www.y-gelli.co.uk

Rhiwiau Isaf
tel 01248 681143
rhiwiau@aol.com
www.rhiwiau.co.uk

Conwy

Hostels
YHA Conwy
tel 0845 3719732
www.yha.org.uk

Llandudno Hostel (a short train journey away across the Afon Conwy)
tel 01492 877430info@
llandudnohostel.co.uk
www.llandudnohostel.co.uk

B&Bs/guest houses
Gwynfryn
tel 01492 576733
info@gwynfrynbandb.co.uk
www.bedandbreakfastconwy.co.uk

Bryn Guest House
tel 01492 592449
stay@bryn.org.uk
www.bryn.org.uk

Hotel
Castle Hotel
tel 01492 582800
reservations@castlewales.co.uk
www.castlewales.co.uk

APPENDIX B
Facilities tables

Main route

Place	Distance	Cumulative distance	Facilities
Machynlleth	0	0	Hotels, B&Bs, food shops, train station, buses
Esgairgeiliog Ceinws	4½ miles (7km)	4½ miles (7km)	Pub
Corris	1 mile (1.5km)	5½ miles (9km)	Pub, hostel, café, buses
Aberllefenni	1½ miles (2.5km)	7 miles (11.4km)	Buses
Dolgellau	8½ miles (13.5km)	15½ miles (24.7km)	Hotels, B&Bs, campsite, food shops, pubs, restaurants, information centre
Llanelltyd	1¼ miles (2km)	16½ miles (26.7km)	Buses
Coed y Brenin Visitor Centre (1 mile off-route)	6¼ miles (10km)	23 miles (36.7km)	Café and shop
Trawsfynydd	6½ miles (10.5km)	29½ miles (47.3km)	Inn, B&B, campsite, food shop, buses
Bryn Glâs	7¾ miles (12.5km)	37¼ miles (59.8km)	Buses, train station (at Llandecwyn)
Penrhyndeudraeth	1¼ miles (2km)	38½ miles (61.8km)	B&B, buses, train station, pub, café, food shops
Croesor	5 miles (8km)	43½ miles (69.8km)	Café
Beddgelert	4½ miles (7km)	48 miles (76.8km)	Hotels, B&Bs, campsite, food shops, cafés, pubs, buses, information centre

Place	Distance	Cumulative distance	Facilities
Bethania	3½ miles (5.5km)	51½ miles (82.3km)	Café, campsite
Pont Rufeinig	7½ miles (12km)	59 miles (94.3km)	Train station
Dolwyddelan	1¾ miles (3.1km)	60¾ miles (97.4km)	Hotel, bunkhouse, pub, food shop, buses, train station
Capel Curig	4½ miles (7km)	65¼ miles (104.4km)	Cafés, outdoor shops, pubs, buses, hotels, B&Bs, hostel, food shop
Idwal Cottage	6¼ miles (10km)	71½ miles (114.4km)	Hostel, café
Bethesda	4¾ miles (8.1km)	76¼ miles (122.5km)	B&B, bunkhouse, restaurants, food shop, cafés, buses
Llanfairfechan	11¾ (19km)	88 miles (141.5km)	B&Bs, campsite, bunkhouse, food shops, train station, buses, pub
Conwy	9¼ (14.6km)	97 miles (156km)	Hotels, B&Bs, hostel, food shops, information centre, buses, train station, pubs
Mountain route			
Machynlleth	0	0	Hotels, B&Bs, food shops, train station, buses
Pennal (½ mile off-route)	4½ miles (7km)	4½ miles (7km)	Pub, food shop, buses
Abergynolwyn	7½ miles (12.5km)	12 miles (19.5km)	Pub, buses, B&B, campsite
Dolgellau	14¾ (23.6km)	26¾ miles (43.1km)	Hotels, B&Bs, campsite, food shops, pubs, restaurants, information centre

Place	Distance	Cumulative distance	Facilities
Llanelltyd	1¼ miles (2km)	28 miles (45.1km)	Buses
Trawsfynydd	15¼ miles (24.6km)	43¼ miles (69.7km)	Inn, B&B, campsite, food shop, buses
Bryn Glâs	10½ miles (17km)	53¾ miles (86.7km)	Buses, train station (at Llandecwyn)
Penrhyndeudraeth	1¼ miles (2km)	55 miles (88.7km)	B&B, buses, train station, pub, café, food shops
Beddgelert	15¾ miles (25.2km)	70¾ miles (113.9km)	Hotels, B&Bs, campsite, food shops, cafés, pubs, buses, information centre
Bethania	3½ miles (5.5km)	74¼ miles (119.4km)	Café, campsite
Snowdon summit	4½ miles (7km)	78¾ miles (126.4km)	Café, train station, shop
Pen-y-Pass	3¼ miles (5.4km)	82 miles (131.8km)	Hostel, cafés, buses
Capel Curig	9½ miles (15.5km)	91½ miles (147.3km)	Cafés, outdoor shops, pubs, buses, hotels, B&Bs, hostel, food shop
Bethesda	12¾ miles (20.4km)	104¼ miles (167.7km)	B&B, bunkhouse, restaurants, food shop, cafés, buses
Conwy	18 miles (28.7km)	122 miles (196km)	Hotels, B&Bs, hostel, food shops, information centre, buses, train station, pubs

APPENDIX C
Useful contacts

Public transport information
Traveline Cymru
tel 0300 200 2233
www.traveline.cymru

Arrive Trains Wales
www.arrivatrainswales.co.uk

Local taxi companies
Machynlleth
Peter's Taxi
tel 01654 749065

Mach Taxis
tel 01654 702048

Dolgellau
Derek's Taxis
tel 01341 422409

Cader Cabs
tel 07766 983103

Trasfynydd
Nev-S Taxis
tel 07768 221709

John's Coaches
tel 01766 831781

Penrhyndeudraeth
B&M Taxis
tel 01766 770851

Betws-y-Coed
Lyn-An Taxis
tel 01745 860656

Bethesda
Penrhyn Cars
tel 01248 600072

A1 Cars
tel 01248 602111

Conwy
Castle Cabs
tel 01492 593398

Roger's Taxis
tel 01492 572224

General tourist information
Visit Snowdonia
tel 01341 281485
www.visitsnowdonia.info

Snowdonia National Park Authority
tel 01766 770274
www.eryri-npa.gov.uk

Wales Directory
www.walesdirectory.co.uk

Local tourist information
Machynlleth
www.machynlleth.net

Visit Mid Wales(reaches roughly as far
north as the Vale of Ffestiniog)
www.visitmidwales.co.uk

Dolgellau
www.dolgellau-snowdonia.co.uk

Trawsfynydd
trawsfynydd.com

Porthmadog (near Penrhyndeudraeth)
tel 01766 512981
www.porthmadog.co.uk

Beddgelert
www.beddgelerttourism.com

Betws-y-Coed (near Dolwyddelan)
www.betws-y-coed.co.uk

Capel Curig
www.visitcapel.co.uk

Conwy and North Wales
tel 01492 577577
www.visitllandudno.org.uk

Weather updates
BBC Weather
www.bbc.co.uk/weather

Mountain Weather Information Service
(Snowdonia)
www.mwis.org.uk/
english-welsh-forecast/SD

Met Office Mountain Weather
(Snowdonia)
www.metoffice.gov.uk/public/weather/
mountain-forecasts/snowdonia

Mountain Rescue
Call 999 and ask for police

APPENDIX D

Further reading

WM Condry, *The Snowdonia National Park (New Naturalist series)* (1976), Collins

Paul Gannon, *Rock Trails Snowdonia* (2nd edn 2013), Pesda Press

Gwili Gog, *Understanding Welsh Place Names* (2015 edn), Northern Eye Books

Jim Perrin, *Snowdon* (1st edn 2013), Gomer

Mike Raine, *Nature of Snowdonia* (2009), Pesda Press

Michael Senior, *Eryri: The story of Snowdonia* (2011), Llygad Gwalch Cyf

Merfyn Williams and Jeremy Moore, *Snowdonia: The Official National Park Guide* (2000), David & Charles

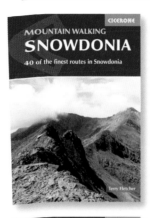
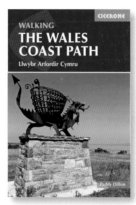
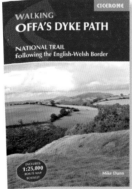

Walking – Trekking – Mountaineering – Climbing – Cycling

Over 40 years, Cicerone have built up an outstanding collection of over 300 guides, inspiring all sorts of amazing adventures.

Every guide comes from extensive exploration and research by our expert authors, all with a passion for their subjects. They are frequently praised, endorsed and used by clubs, instructors and outdoor organisations.

All our titles can now be bought as **e-books**, **ePubs** and **Kindle** files and we also have an online magazine – **Cicerone Extra** – with features to help cyclists, climbers, walkers and trekkers choose their next adventure, at home or abroad.

Our website shows any **new information** we've had in since a book was published. Please do let us know if you find anything has changed, so that we can publish the latest details. On our **website** you'll also find great ideas and lots of detailed information about what's inside every guide and you can buy **individual routes** from many of them online.

It's easy to keep in touch with what's going on at Cicerone by getting our monthly **free e-newsletter**, which is full of offers, competitions, up-to-date information and topical articles. You can subscribe on our home page and also follow us on **Facebook** and **Twitter** or dip into our **blog**.

Cicerone – the very best guides for exploring the world.

CICERONE

2 Police Square Milnthorpe Cumbria LA7 7PY
Tel: 015395 62069 info@cicerone.co.uk
www.cicerone.co.uk and **www.cicerone-extra.com**